A. Secretaire cabinet, veneered with zebra wood. Mounted with Egyptian masks and feet in brass. The glass doors backed with watercolour landscape drawings signed Baynes, 1808.

Victoria and Albert Museum

REGENCY FURNITURE

1800 to 1830

REGENCY FURNITURE

1800 to 1830

by

CLIFFORD MUSGRAVE

FABER AND FABER

24 Russell Square

London

First published in 1961
by Faber and Faber Limited
24 Russell Square London W.C.1
Second revised edition 1970
Printed in Great Britain
by Robert MacLehose & Co. Ltd Glasgow
All rights reserved

SBN 571 04694 0

For

ROGER AND BEATRICE

FOREWORD

In the present work a more exact and penetrating stylistic analysis has been attempted than ever before in respect of the furniture of the Regency period.

Special thought has been devoted not only to the development of styles and movements of taste during the Regency period, but to the historical, social and psychological influences that brought them about.

The question of French influences has been newly studied, especially regarding its earlier phases, but also in its later manifestations, including that pervasive trend of early nineteenth century taste, the revival of the Louis Quatorze style, though not to the extent of overlooking English originality, individuality and fantasy.

Fresh attention has also been bestowed upon those familiar figures in the history of Regency styles, Henry Holland and Thomas Hope, in an attempt to banish some of the confusion which has existed in respect of these two pioneers, and to aid towards a fuller understanding of their influence.

In considering the great changes of fashion that occurred between 1811 and 1815, some thought has been given to a neglected phase of taste, the revival about that time of a pure though unpedantic classical style.

As well as surveying the movements of style and taste, the book is a reference work for details of design, and is thus intensely practical, and it should be useful not only to the historian of style, but to the collector, connoisseur, and interior decorator.

In such a work as this it is inevitable that a certain amount of standard information is repeated, but it is hoped that where this occurs some fresh light may be shed into corners long thought familiar.

J.L.

PREFACE TO SECOND EDITION

For this new edition the text has been completely corrected and revised, and the results of recent researches and discoveries have been incorporated.

P.T.

ACKNOWLEDGEMENTS

The gracious permission of H.M. The Queen for me to carry out research in the Royal Archives and Royal Library at Windsor is gratefully acknowledged.

For special help I am indebted to Mr. R. Mackworth-Young, M.V.O., the Queen's Librarian; Miss A. Scott-Elliott, M.V.O., Keeper of the Prints and Drawings; Miss E. Price-Hill, Registrar of the Royal Archives; Mr. Francis J. B. Watson, M.V.O., F.S.A., Surveyor of the Queen's Works of Art; Mr. Geoffrey de Bellaigue, M.V.O., Assistant Surveyor; Mr. Peter Thornton, Keeper of the Department of Woodwork, Victoria and Albert Museum; Mme. Denise Ledoux-Lebard, author of *Les ébénistes parisiens, 1795–1830*; Mme. Louis Amic, of the Musée des Arts Décoratifs, The Louvre; Mr. I. O. Chance, Chairman of Messrs. Christie's; Major Simon Whitbread, of Southill Park, Beds.; Mr. L. G. G. Ramsey, F.S.A., Editor of *The Connoisseur*; Mr. John Lowe, formerly of the Victoria and Albert Museum; Mr. John Blairman for notes on Thomas Hope; my colleagues Mr. H. Ferris Brazenor, F.R.N.S., Deputy Director, Royal Pavilion Estate, and Mr. Derek L. Rogers, Assistant Curator, Brighton Art Gallery and Museum; and Miss Patricia Ranger, my secretary.

I owe an immeasurable debt of gratitude to my wife for her help and encouragement, and to my sons Roger and Stephen, the former for discovering various early reference works, and the latter for making the photographs from original design books which are used in the work.

My thanks are due to the following for permission to reproduce photographs:

The Lord Chamberlain for furniture in the Royal collections: Nos. 2A, 2B, 28A, 28B, 47B, 63, 74; Brighton Corporation for furniture in the Royal Pavilion: Nos. 3, 18, 25, 39, 39A, 42B, 44, 45A, 45B, 46A, 59, 62, 73, 76A, 77B, 81, 84, 85, 93; and at Preston Manor: Nos. 46B, 50B, 53; The Board of Admiralty for the Dolphin Furniture: No. 11; The National Trust for the Dorneywood furniture: No. 27; The Victoria and Albert Museum: Nos. 13, 17, 91, and two colour plates; Lady Birley: No. 10; Mr. Paul Channon, M.P.: No. 26; Mr. W. B. Henderson: No. 72; the Hon. Mrs. Ionides: Nos. 24B, 38B, 89B; Mrs. Clifford Musgrave: No. 39B; and Major S. Whitbread for the Southill furniture: Nos. 4B, 5, 6, 29, 30, 31.

For help in providing information and for supplying scarce reference works I am grateful to Mr. A. H. Hall, F.L.A., City Librarian, The Guildhall, London; Mr. C. M. Jackson, F.L.A., Borough Librarian, Shoreditch; Mr. C. S. Minto, F.L.A., City Librarian, and Mr. J. W. Cockburn, F.L.A., Depute Librarian, Edinburgh; Mr. Leslie Godden; Mr. K. Smith, F.R.E.S., F.L.A., City Librarian, Carlisle; Miss F. M. Green, F.L.A., Borough Librarian, Brentford and Chiswick; and to Miss M. C. Watson, F.L.A., Chief Assistant, Reference Library, Brighton, and her colleagues.

I owe a very great debt of gratitude to the following who have so very generously provided photographs: H. Blairman and Sons, Ltd.: Nos. 12A, 12B, 14A, 14B, 15A, 16B, 19, 20A, 21, 22A, 35, 38A, 39A, 43A, 50A, 55, 57, 67A, 68, 69, 78B, 86, 87, 88A, 90A, 95B, 96; Mr. J. W. Blanchard: Nos. 54, 56, 76B; Gregory & Co.: No. 67B; M. Harris and Sons: Nos. 17, 34A, 51, 52A, 60, 61, 70, 78A, 83, 88B; Harrods, Ltd.: Nos. 34B, 66A, 75; Jeremy, Ltd.: No. 74; Mr. Leonard Knight: Nos. 66B, 82; Maple and Co., Ltd.: Nos. 80A, 80B; Trevor-Antiques of Brighton: No. 85; Frank Partridge and Sons, Ltd.: Nos. 48, 71; Restall, Brown and Clennell, Ltd.: Nos. 79B, 90B, 95A; Temple Williams, Ltd.: Nos. 8A, 8B, 20B, 22A, 22B, 24B, 36, 37, 41A, 42A, 64, 65, 79A, 89A, 94.

Grateful acknowledgement is made to Fine Art Photography, Ltd., for permission to reproduce the two colour photographs of the Royal Pavilion, and I would also thank the following for great kindness in supplying prints of their photographs: A. C. Cooper, Ltd., for Nos. 2A, 2B; Frank Dobinson, M.P.A., P.D.A., Brighton, for Nos. 1, 3, 10, 18, 21, 25, 38B, 39A, 39B, 42B, 43B, 44, 45A, 45B, 47A, 52B, 58, 59, 62, 76A, 77B, 81, 106, 113, 123; Fine Art Engravers, Ltd., for Nos. 4B, 5, 6, 11, 15B, 26, 27, 28A, 28B, 29, 30, 31, 46A, 46B, 47B, 50B, 53, 63, 72, 73, 74, 76B, 77A; Raymond Fortt, A.I.B.P., for Nos. 4A, 7, 8A, 8B, 12A, 17, 20B, 22A, 22B, 34A, 36, 37, 41A, 42A, 49, 50A, 51, 52A, 57, 60, 61, 64, 66B, 67B, 68, 69, 70, 78A, 78B, 79A, 82, 83, 86, 88A, 89A, 94; E. & N. Gibbs, for Nos. 12B, 14A, 14B, 15A, 16B, 19, 20A, 35, 38A, 40, 41B, 43A, 55, 65, 67A, 71, 87, 88B, 90A, 95B, 96; L. H. Hillyard, for Nos. 34B, 66A, 75; Ravenna Studios, for Nos. 80A, 80B; F. Simms, Brighton, for Nos. 16A, 24A, 24B, 54, 56, 84; Victoria and Albert Museum, for Nos. 13, 17, 91.

CONTENTS

Contents

Contents

Note: Houses marked with an asterisk * are open to the public.

ILLUSTRATIONS

in the text

The five conversation pieces by Henry Moses are from engravings in *Designs for Modern Costume*, 1823, and illustrate articles of furniture shown in Hope's *Household Furniture and Interior Decoration*, 1807.

ILLUSTRATIONS

(plates)

COLOUR PLATES

MONOCHROME PLATES

at the end of the book

INTRODUCTION

Interest in furniture of the Regency period has been growing steadily during the last thirty years, and the present work has been written in response to the need for a book giving a more complete and up-to-date account of the subject than has been published hitherto, and embodying the results of modern research.

In the present work it has been thought desirable to cover the whole field of Regency furniture, dwelling strongly upon the simpler and more domestic types, which the ordinary reader is likely to possess, at the same time endeavouring to be useful to the collector and connoisseur, and to the antique dealer and interior decorator. Consideration has therefore been given also to furniture of pronounced stylistic character and fine quality.

Better opportunities exist to-day for seeing furniture of the most splendid sort, as well as of the more simple domestic kind, now that so many more country houses are open to the public than was the case even a few years ago, and that furniture collections in museums, both of London and the provinces have been so greatly enlarged.

The popularity of Regency furniture steadily developed after its restoration in the 1920's, little effected by vagaries of fashion, and since the last war the vogue for it has become more and more firmly established. Its suitability for modern homes and its appeal to present-day tastes is based not so much on fashionable whims, as on a number of considerations which are part of the affinity of the Regency age with modern times. The Regency age was a time of rapid development in ideas of functional house-planning for comfort, convenience and pleasure; the open informal arrangement of rooms, with the consequent need for furniture to be light and small enough to be easily moved about; the large expanses of window; the fondness for elaborate curtaining and for wall-to-wall carpeting; the cultivation of indoor plants and the breaking down of barriers between house and garden; and the furniture then used has been found admirably suited to modern interiors in which these ideas have been more completely realized.

For a number of years we have been accustomed to using the word 'Regency' not merely to cover the nine years of the constitutional Regency, from 1811 to

1820, when George, Prince of Wales ruled as Prince Regent during the sickness of his father King George III, but to describe the decorative arts that flourished during the first thirty years of the nineteenth century. Especially in considering the origins of Regency furniture the present work considers purchases of the Prince during the whole of his adult life, from the attainment of his majority in 1783 until his death as King George IV in 1830.

The use of the word 'Regency' to describe the furniture and architecture of the period was by no means always common. Margaret Jourdain first used the word in the title of a book in 1923.[1] The term was also used at an early date by the late Sir Albert Richardson, who collected articles of the period in his house at Ampthill, and it was given further early currency by Edward Knoblock, who had collections of furniture both English and French, including articles designed by Thomas Hope, in his house at Clifton Terrace, Brighton, at Beach House, Worthing, and in his rooms in Albany, London. Under the inspiration of Mrs. Dolly Mann,[2] the Regency spirit was carried into the decoration and furnishing of a number of interiors during the years following the First World War, outstandingly in the house of the late Sir Henry Channon M.P., at 5 Belgrave Square. Before that time, the principal fashionable decorators despised anything later than 1800.

It has been stated, possibly not with complete accuracy, that the Regency style was not the style of the Prince Regent. What may perhaps fairly be said is that Regency furniture began and ended with the Regent's own taste — that it began with the furniture he bought as the young Prince of Wales, and culminated in the rich florid taste he favoured in his later years. In its varying aspects Regency furniture expresses many of the widely differing and indeed even contrary qualities of that remarkable age, its grace, simplicity, elegance, robustness and splendour, qualities which made that period one of the richest ever known in the creative arts.

[1] Jourdain, *English Interiors*, 1923. (Full details of works mentioned in the footnotes are given in the Bibliography.) [2] Ronald Fleming, *The Saturday Book*, 1959.

HENRY HOLLAND
FRENCH AND CLASSICAL ORIGINS

The age of Regency furniture may be said to have begun when the Prince of Wales appointed Henry Holland to rebuild and refurbish Carlton House, which was assigned to the Prince as his London establishment upon his coming of age in August 1783. On taking possession the young Prince embarked upon a series of alterations to the building and furnishings that were to continue over forty years, in fact almost until the house was demolished in 1827, when the Prince, who had succeeded to the throne as King George IV in 1820, was having Buckingham Palace built for him by John Nash.

The Prince expressed his resentment against the unsympathetic upbringing he had received from his father by choosing his friends among the leaders of the Whig party, who were then in opposition to the King, and it was doubtless through these friends that the Prince came to choose as his architect, Henry Holland, who held the post until his death in 1806. Holland had been a pupil and assistant of the landscape architect 'Capability' Brown, and married his daughter Bridget. Through his father-in-law Holland was given introductions to an enormous fashionable circle. In 1776 he was employed to design Brooks's club-house in St. James's, the stronghold of the Whigs, and thenceforth all his most important commissions were for the wealthy members of that party, for Lord Palmerston at Broadlands, Lord Spencer at Althorp* and Samuel Whitbread at Southill.

It is no doubt likely that the distinctly French atmosphere which Holland created at Carlton House was pleasing to the Francophil inclinations of his patrons, which have so often been remarked upon, and unquestionably it provided an appropriate setting for the magnificent French furniture of which the Prince was such an ardent collector. In these early days the Prince was accustomed to send Louis Weltje, his general man of affairs, as well as being his 'Clerk of the Kitchen', to buy French furniture at sales held in Paris. On the eve of the Revolution many of the newly impoverished aristocrats were being forced to sell their fine furniture, and afterwards the revolutionary government sold important articles of furniture confiscated from their victims.

Two of the principal agents in supplying furniture to Carlton House were Dominique Daguerre, a *marchand-mercier* who had once been a purveyor of furniture to Louis XVI, and his partner Martin Eloy Lignereux, who in 1793 succeeded to the business in Sloane Street, London. From William Beckford's *Letters from Paris* we learn that before Daguerre came to London he was selling French furniture to English visitors at enormous prices.

There are few bills of furniture-dealers and craftsmen preserved in the Royal Archives which relate to this period, but it is clear from the documents that do exist that the French element was strongly pervasive. Through Daguerre, furniture by the *ébéniste* Georges Jacob was supplied to the Prince, and the extent to which Lignereux provided him with articles from his shop is shown by the fact that in 1795 his demands upon the Prince amounted to £15,000. Another Frenchman mentioned is Francis Hervé, a chair-maker, who is shown as requiring £3,000 to complete the furnishings. Other French names that appear in the accounts for 1783 to 1786 are those of Jean Dominique, 'fondeur', and Louis André Delabrière, painter and decorator, who was also concerned later with Holland's work at the Brighton Pavilion and at Southill.

About this time the famous Chinese Dining-Room was formed at Carlton House which Sheraton describes and illustrates with two drawings in the second edition of his first work, *The Cabinet-Maker and Upholsterer's Drawing Book* published in 1794. Most of the furniture from this room was brought to the Royal Pavilion at Brighton, in 1802, when the neo-classic interior which Holland had created there fifteen years earlier was remodelled with a Chinese scheme of decoration, and these articles form today part of the furnishing of Buckingham Palace.

Two splendid pier-tables, of ebony veneer with ormolu mounts, were important features of the Chinese Drawing-Room. The two tables differ slightly in design. One has supports in the form of Chinese terminal figures (Plate 2A); the other has straight supports, and the opening of the centre portion has decoration in ormolu in the shape of curtain-drapery. There was a magnificent chimney-piece, again flanked by Chinese terminal figures, and a set of chairs, also of ebony and ormolu, with square backs and slender tapering legs, reeded and entwined with snakes.

This furniture has been described by several authorities as designed by Henry Holland,[1] chiefly on the grounds that Holland was responsible for supervising all the furnishing of Carlton House. No bills for these particular articles exist, and there are strong reasons for believing that Henry Holland was not responsible for

[1] See Note 1 (p. 145).

their design, but that they are the work of some French *ébéniste*. With their extreme delicacy of design, and the fine scale of the ormolu decoration, they have a distinctively French character that is very different from the bold and almost sturdy dignity of form we associate with work for which we believe Holland may have been more directly responsible. Many characteristics of the pier-tables are those of that great master and innovator of the Empire style, Adam Weisweiler, one of the favourite *ébénistes* of Marie Antoinette.[1] They are made of ebony, a material of which Weisweiler was especially fond, but which is not used in any furniture associated with Holland; the bronze terminal figures resemble those made by Gouthière for Weisweiler,[2] and the spirally decorated tapering feet *en toupie* are of a kind often used by this *ébéniste*. He was closely associated with Dominique Daguerre and Lignereux, for it was through the former that Weisweiler supplied an important bookcase to Holland for Lord Spencer at Althorp.[3] It is thus extremely probable that it was one of these two purveyors who supplied the pier-tables to Carlton House.[4]

Whoever was the designer, what is important is that in expressing some of the most characteristic forms and features of English domestic furniture which were in vogue during the next fifty years they may be said to represent the precursors in this country of the Regency style in furniture. In these pieces we see clearly the Louis Seize spirit with which the furniture associated with Holland, and a great deal of Regency furniture generally, came to be infused. Both pairs have straight-fronted marble tops with bowed ends, repeating the shape of the curved open shelves below — a form characteristic of the *commodes ouvertes* of the Louis Seize period designed by such *ébénistes* as Carlin and Benemann as well as Weisweiler. Henry Holland adopted the form for the open end-shelves of the large dining-room sideboards which he supplied to Althorp*, and the design persisted as one of the most favoured and distinctive of the Regency period (Plates 49, 50A, 51, 54).

The pronounced French character of Holland's architectural interiors that is one of the most notable features of his work seems to have derived from the study of designs by French architects such as Peyre, Pierre Patte and Gondoin,[5] and possibly by Desgodetz. Holland himself visited Paris in 1785, and it is believed that during this time he visited Versailles. By the latter year not only had the style of Louis Seize reached full development, but as will be seen later, all the essential forms and motifs of what was eventually to become the Empire style.

[1] See Note 2 (p. 145). [2] Illustrated in Clifford Smith, *Buckingham Palace*, 1931. Plate 129.
[3] Watson, *Southill*, 1951. [4] See Note 3 (p. 146). [5] Stroud, *Henry Holland*, 1966.

It is highly probable that Holland also received a great deal of inspiration from the remarkable band of French furnishers, designers and craftsmen he had gathered round himself at Carlton House, and who worked for him at Southill and Althorp, as well as from the French pieces that he obtained for these places. The superb black laquer commode in the Yellow Drawing-Room at Althorp, the matching *encoignures* of which bear the stamp of C. C. Saunier, was bought by Holland at the D'Alberg sale through Daguerre in 1791,[1] and alone would have provided a model for his re-interpretations of the Louis Seize style in the pier-commode and chiffoniers (Plate 6) that he designed for Southill.

The design of some mahogany and gilt settees which were supplied for the entrance hall of Carlton House about 1794[2] may be ascribed to Holland with some confidence. Their scrolled backs, square tapering legs and gilt *guilloche* ornament reveal Louis Seize influence, but the scroll-shaped arm-rests anticipate one of the most characteristic Regency developments. In the absence of direct evidence, their attribution to Holland rests upon the character of their design, which possesses the broad simplicity and refinement of the furniture he later provided for Southill. The same spirit exists also in the settees (Plate 2B) and chairs which were supplied to the Prince for the Brighton Pavilion* in 1802 by his principal firm of cabinet-makers, then trading under the name of Elward, Marsh and Tatham, Upholders, of Mount Street. The general form of these seats is similar to those made for Carlton House, but the front legs of the Pavilion settees and chairs now show the sweeping concave curve that was soon to become one of the most distinctive marks of Regency character (Plates 12A, 12B, 39A, 39B, 40).

Holland's influence in furniture is generally admitted to be seen in its finest and most mature form in the articles he provided for Southill, the home of the Whig politician Mr. Samuel Whitbread, while it was being rebuilt and refurnished during a number of years from 1796 onwards. At first the expenditure on furniture was low, but in 1798 it rose to over £2,000, and remained high for several years, reaching a maximum of nearly £4,000 in 1802. In 1806 Holland died, and by 1807 this expenditure had declined to £100. In the following years it rose again to nearly £1,000 a year until the death of Samuel Whitbread II in 1815.

These fluctuations probably represent the general pattern of spending during the years up to the French restoration; high in the early boom-years of the century, low during the preoccupations and austerities of the final phases of the war, and high again as a new era set in with the decline and fall of Napoleon.

[1] C. Hussey, *Country Life*, 26 May 1960.   [2] Illustrated in Clifford Smith, Plate 107.

No significant purchases of furniture were made after the death of Samuel Whitbread. Upon this event an inventory was taken of the contents of Southill, and it records all the furniture existing at the time.

The furniture purchases for Southill, ranging as they do from 1796 to 1815, cover a period which knew several important changes of style, and the question arises as to the extent to which Holland himself was responsible for the design of the moveables. The only furniture drawings from his own hand known to survive are for architectural fixtures.[1] It is known also that he received £200 in 1801 as 'commission on furniture'. As with the Carlton House articles, there is no absolute certainty that he actually designed any of the furniture which is so generally regarded as an expression of his great genius, but it is inconceivable that for an interior of such exquisite delicacy and artistry Holland should not have devoted the utmost thought to the character of the furniture and given the clearest indications for its design, at least for that supplied up to his death in 1806, and probably for a number of years after. Indeed much of the Southill furniture possesses the unmistakable qualities of rich simplicity and distinction that are found in his architectural work.

The spirit with which the earlier furniture at Southill is infused is of the restrained classical richness of the Louis Seize manner rather than the gaunt, ungilded severity of the *Directoire* style upon which it is so often said to be based. All the lines and motifs which it displays were established in France years before the Directory.[2]

This French character, which is embodied also in the later designs of Thomas Sheraton, forms the basis of much of the Regency style. It presents two aspects, that are shown in the various features of the earlier articles at Southill. Firstly, the freely adapted romantic classicism of the Louis Seize manner, a style which came into being with the furniture made by Delanois for Madame du Barry's Château de Louveciennes in 1771. Many details of the style had probably been anticipated by Robert Adam as much as ten years earlier, and were not to survive the century, but others, such as the tapering and fluted, or turned columns at the corners of cabinets, and peg-top feet were to become important features of design in England (Plates 2A, 6, 48, 49, 50A, 51, 54, 57).

The second phase was that of the severely correct archaeological classicism of the furniture details drawn from Etruscan wall-paintings, Greek vases and other sources of antique inspiration, which characterized the later days of the Louis

---

[1] Sketchbook in R.I.B.A. See also Note 4 (p. 146).   [2] See Note 5 (p. 146).

Seize period. This phase was initiated with the furniture which Georges Jacob supplied for Marie Antoinette's *Laiterie* at Rambouillet in 1787, to designs by Hubert Robert,[1] and the articles which he made to the designs of the painter J. L. David for his studio in 1788.[2]

In a sense the latter were studio properties, and they appear in such paintings by David as the *Oath of the Horatii*, the *Return of Brutus*, the *Cupid and Psyche*, and the unfinished portrait of Madame Recamier seated upon a couch.[3] But the studio properties became symbols of new aspirations towards austere ideals of ancient virtue, and the models of a style that was firstly to clothe the revolutionary philosophy and then to serve as the trappings of imperialistic dominion.

The forms and motifs of the Empire style were thus fully developed before the Revolution in 1789, and as Mr. F. J. B. Watson has said:[4]

'From this time forward there is no essential break in the development of French decorative styles, at any rate till after the fall of Napoleon. . . . What really differentiates Empire furniture (and decoration generally) from pre-Revolutionary examples is the inferiority of its craftsmanship and materials.'

The 'Etruscan'[5] phase of the Louis Seize style is conveyed especially in such features as the sweeping lines of the legs of the gilt chairs at Southill, in the scrolling of their arms and in the 'crozier' or scroll-form of their backs (Plates 3, 5). Earlier Louis Seize influence appears in the tapering fluted front legs of the chairs, and a distinctive minor Gallic touch is the use in one of the articles of a small panel of *pietra dura*, a material of which Weisweiler was especially fond. Other important details such as the tapering octagonal fluted columns of the pier-commode and chiffoniers (Plate 6), and their vase-shaped feet, while based on Louis Seize models by such craftsmen as Weisweiler and Lannuier, display a simplification of design in a robust and original manner in which we sense the expression of an English mind. Among the earliest pieces must no doubt be counted the famous gilt arm-chairs of the drawing-room (Plate 3) with scrolled arm-rests, fluted front-legs and the bolt-head decoration which is found also in the accompanying sofas (Plate 5). Other chairs, from Mrs. Whitbread's room, with tapering, carved front legs and 'wrapped' palm-leaf decoration (Plate 3) may probably also be

---

[1] *Connaissance des Arts*, May 1958.

[2] Watson, Catalogue of furniture in the Wallace Collection, 1958.

[3] Delécluze, *Louis David, son école et son temps*, 1855. pp. 20–1.

[4] Watson, letter in *The Times Literary Supplement*, 10 July 1953. See also the same author's Catalogue of furniture in the Wallace Collection.

[5] See Note 6 (p. 146).

assigned to the period from 1796, when Holland's work at Southill began, to about 1800. The splendid chiffoniers from the same room have much of the same spirit, and may have been installed by 1800, the date when this room was substantially complete, as we know from a letter written in that year by the Reverend Samuel Johnes.[1]

In the earlier Southill furniture we see not only characteristics of French design, but a number of new decorative themes which had been supplied to Holland by his young assistant, Charles Heathcote Tatham. Having entered Holland's office at the age of nineteen, in 1795 his master sent him to Rome for two years or so with an allowance of £60 a year, to pursue studies in classical design. Tatham sent home to his master a number of drawings of ancient Roman designs (Figs. 2, 11) and also some of Egyptian character, antedating those which appeared in the works of Sheraton, Thomas Hope and George Smith seven years and more later. Thomas Hope attempted in his celebrated book to apply the classical and Egyptian styles to the furniture of everyday life with archaeological exactitude (pp. 45–53), but in the earlier furniture at Southill the new classical elements appear with an ease and grace that is in contrast to the frigid accuracy of Hope's designs, and to the ponderous ugliness of many productions of the later Regency.

Tatham published many of his drawings made in Rome in a folio volume in 1799 under the title *Examples of Ancient Ornamental Architecture*, and in this work one sees several of the characteristic themes of furniture decoration found not only at Southill, but which mark the whole of the Regency period. Other editions of the work followed in 1803, 1810 and 1826, the last of these being republished as late as 1843.

In seeking out the sources of ancient decorative detail Tatham did very much what the Adam brothers had done some thirty or forty years earlier, but the significance of his work for Regency furniture was that he paved the way for the more strictly archaeological approach to furniture and design which Thomas Hope later pursued, and it was in recognition of this contribution which Tatham made, and of his work for Holland, that the architect Joseph Gwilt was able to write in 1842,[2] 'to him perhaps more than any other person, may be attributed the rise of the Anglo-Greek style which still prevails. . . .'[3]

Some of the principal motifs from Tatham's designs that we find appearing

[1] Quoted by Watson in *Southill*.
[2] The Architectural Publication Society's *Dictionary*, 1842.
[3] See also p. 91, and Note 7 (p. 146).

throughout the Regency are such features as the Chimera monopodium (some-times with the torso emerging from an acanthus leaf) (Fig. 2); the table of circular form carried on three monopodia supports (Plate 4A); cross-framed stools (Plates 14A, 15A); lion-masks with rings as ornaments for tables (Plates 30, 31, 72, 78B); cabinet-supports in the form of terminal figures; and the pedestal of a table or candelabrum rising like a shaft from acanthus leaves (Plates 31, 72).

As with the furniture supplied to the Prince of Wales at Carlton House from 1795, the principal cabinet-makers employed by Holland at Southill were the firm of Marsh and Tatham, of 13 Mount Street, London. In 1795 they were described as William Marsh and Co., Upholders,[1] and two years later they are mentioned as Elward, Marsh & Co., Upholsterers. The name Tatham first appears in 1802, on the bill for supplying the mahogany hall settees and chairs for the Brighton Pavilion,[2] and as Elward, Marsh and Tatham they supplied very many articles of furniture of different kinds to Carlton House, the Brighton Pavilion and Southill. All the work supplied by them of whatever date, is marked by rare qualities of design and craftsmanship.

Although the interior at Southill was substantially complete by 1802, when expenditure reached its peak, a number of important pieces must have been supplied after Holland's death, for large sums continued to be spent. These articles will be considered more fully in a later chapter (see page 74). Among them may possibly be included the circular drawing-room tables (Plates 6, 31), and the straight-ended writing-table (Plate 30). These embody many of the characteristic themes found in Charles Tatham's designs, and may owe their design more or less directly to him.

The elder partner in the cabinet-making firm, which had become Tatham and Bailey in 1809, was in fact Charles's brother, Thomas Tatham. He died in Brighton on 1 January 1818, leaving a fortune of £60,000.[3]

Some articles of furniture similar to those at Southill were at Hartwell House, Buckinghamshire, until 1938, when most of the contents were sold. Hartwell, which was rented to Louis XVIII of France during his exile in this country, was one of the properties of William Lee Antonie of Colworth, a friend of Samual Whitbread's, and a fellow-Whig who stood with him three times as M.P. for Bedford.

A set of gilt arm-chairs now in the Royal Pavilion Collection (Plate 5) are similar to some of Louis Seize 'Etruscan' character at Southill (Plate 3), and the

---

[1] Duchy of Cornwall bill.   [2] Royal Archives.   [3] *Gentleman's Magazine*, January 1818, p. 88.

logic of events, as well as of style, suggests that they were most probably bought between 1796, when Holland began furnishing for Whitbread, and 1799, when William Lee Antonie died. They were presumably first used at Colworth, and later moved to Hartwell.

The octagonal library table which was at Hartwell (Plate 72) like the large tables at Southill (Plate 31) bears the marks of later style and might well have been bought about 1815, when Lee's nephew, John Fiott (1783–1866) a collector of antiquities and 'man of science'[1] inherited Colworth and assumed the name of his uncle. Fiott inherited Hartwell also in 1827, and it was probably at this time that the furniture was brought from Colworth. As well as these and other articles,[2] a commode-chiffonier, one of a pair once at Headfort in Ireland, illustrated by Margaret Jourdain,[3] and various other examples in the Southill manner have appeared from time to time in recent years. In one of these (Plate 57) small panels of painted porcelain serve the same decorative function as insets of *pietra dura* in articles by Weisweiler and in a small occasional table at Southill.

Classical and French influences are evident also in the superb furniture made for Sir William Colt Hoare at Stourhead,* Wiltshire, by Thomas Chippendale the younger (1749 to 1822) from 1795 to 1820. These articles are mostly described in the accounts which are preserved in the Library, and are well illustrated in Jourdain[4] and in Edwards.[5]

The principal early purchases were made in 1802, and include the elegant arm-chairs of satinwood which are to be seen in various rooms of the house, having broad convex yoke-backs with cross-bars in Grecian style, and slender tapering turned legs of Louis Seize influence. Similar chairs are to be found in several private collections in other houses, and were possibly also acquired from Chippendale.

[1] *Dictionary of National Biography.*
[2] Hartwell House Sale Catalogue, July 1938.
[3] Jourdain, *Regency Furniture*, 1965, Fig. 5.
[4] *Regency Furniture.*
[5] *Dictionary of English Furniture*, 1954.

THOMAS SHERATON
AND THE NEW INFLUENCES

While these movements in the design of furniture were taking place in the Royal palaces and in great houses, furniture for middle-class houses was still being made during the early years of the new century in the tradition established by the earlier design books of Thomas Sheraton, and even under the now rapidly declining influence of the Adam scheme of decorative motifs. These had been summed up in the designs of George Hepplewhite in *The Cabinet-Maker and Upholsterer's Guide* published in 1788 after his death, and in other editions of his work which came out in 1789 and 1794.

Hepplewhite deserves mention in a work on Regency furniture if only because he popularized the device of the three Prince of Wales's feathers used as a design for the back splat of chairs, and as a motif for wood inlay at the tops of table legs, and he claimed in the *Guide* that one of his chair designs had been 'executed with good effect for His Royal Highness', although there is no mention of his name in the Royal accounts.

The tendencies existing up to the end of the century were chiefly expressed in *The Cabinet-Maker and Upholsterer's Drawing Book*, by Thomas Sheraton. It was published in three parts, with an appendix, from 1791 to 1794. The first two parts consisted of elaborate treatises on geometry and perspective, subjects which Sheraton considered had been grievously neglected by craftsmen previously. Part III of the work contained designs which Sheraton explained were 'intended to exhibit the present taste of furniture, and at the same time to give the workman some assistance in the manufacturing part of it'. Once again this was something that had been neglected in earlier furniture design books. A second edition was brought out in 1794, and a third in 1802. It is now generally realized that Sheraton himself did not manufacture furniture to his designs,[1] and although he had been for many years a journeyman cabinet-maker, since 1793 he had supported himself and his wife and children 'by his exertions as an author'.[2]

[1] M. Jourdain and R. Edwards, *Georgian Cabinet-Makers*, 1946.   [2] *Gentleman's Magazine*, November 1806.

B. A Regency drawing-room at the Royal Pavilion, Brighton. Trafalgar chairs, c. 1805, gilt arm-chairs of Southill type, c. 1800, and brass-inlaid drawing-room tables, c. 1820.

In Sheraton's *Drawing Book* and its appendices we see the marks of his style which survived until about 1800, such familiar features of the pure Sheraton manner as the slender, square tapering leg, and arms of chairs set high, joining the arm-stumps at right-angles, or with a small flattened scroll, or sometimes with a continuous downward curve. Highly distinctive also of the earlier Sheraton style was the inlay of contrasting woods, especially of sycamore or mahogany on satinwood, frequently in the form of a shell in the centre of a table top or tray, or of a fan-like shape in the corners of a table or box. All these motifs died out more or less quickly in the new century.

An important element in the *Drawing Book* that persisted in the developing tradition was the use of reeding, or narrow convex ribbing, as distinct from hollow fluting, for the legs of tables and chairs, and for the edges of shelves and uprights (Plates 8A, 8B, 9B, 40, 41B, 43A, 67A). Another continuing feature was the use of splayed 'claw' feet for tripod and table-supports, in all the three forms of a concave, convex or double curve in which it reached the height of delicacy during the last years of the eighteenth century.

After 1800 Sheraton's typical early splayed foot for legs of tables or tripod-stands changed from the form in which it was supported underneath on a short stump to a brass metal shoe covering the end of the splayed leg. At first the shoe was square and plain, but later it was made in the shape of a lion-paw, or decorated in the form of an acanthus leaf or similar ornament (Plates 8A, 8B, 58, 59). Sheraton also adopted the turned tapering cabinet-foot of French origin, the *pied en toupie*, which sometimes had a twisted decoration of a round metal rod set in a spiral groove (Plates 2A, 48, 49, 50A, 51). Other early Sheraton themes that lived into the next age were kidney-shaped table tops, and concave or convex fronts and rounded ends for writing-desks and chests-of-drawers (Plate 7).

In 1803 Sheraton published *The Cabinet Dictionary*, and from 1804 to 1806 *The Cabinet-Maker, Upholsterer and General Artist's Encyclopaedia*, but the author's death in the latter year prevented the completion of the work. These two volumes of Sheraton's are the ones that have most significance for our period, for in them are embodied many of the characteristic features of the furniture of the Regency age until about 1812. Indeed, the popularity of his designs was given new life by the publication in that year of a volume of designs from the *Dictionary* and *Encyclopaedia* entitled *Designs for Household Furniture*.

Sheraton made no claims to originality in his designs, but there are evident in his work a distinctive elegance and refinement that are the easily recognized marks of his style. Above all, he was sensitive to the changing moods of taste, and his two later books were a signpost to the future styles rather than a statement of existing trends.

Quick to sense the fluctuations of fashionable taste, in his *Cabinet Dictionary* Sheraton gives fuller expression to the tendencies which had become evident in recent years in the refurnishing of Carlton House and Southill. He had clearly made good use of his visit to the former place in 1793. This work is in fact the first crystallization of the Regency style in an English publication. The Grecian taste which was partly the basis of the new mode was very different from the free adaptations of classical themes found in the work of Robert Adam and the neo-Classic school of the late eighteenth century. The labours of Charles Heathcote Tatham in copying the designs of Roman and Greek antiquities in Italy, and the appeal of the classical ideals of order and discipline for the official patrons of art in France during the revolutionary period had focused new attention upon the decorative motifs of the ancient world, and they were now being used with a greater historical exactitude, though still in a state of adaptation to traditional forms, and not with the rigidity that was to develop in a few years time in the designs of Thomas Hope. The classical inspiration at this time, that became increasingly fashionable in France and Italy from the time of the revolution onwards, derived partly from the engravings of antiquities published by Piranesi in Rome about the middle of the century. Their effect in France was to some extent stimulated by the engravings being profusely reprinted from the original plates, which were brought to Paris by Piranesi's sons in 1789, after their father's death.[1]

Much greater influence was probably exercised by that encyclopaedic work of the Comte de Caylus, the *Recueil d'antiquités égyptiennes, étrusques, grecques et romaines* published in a series of seven volumes from 1752 onwards. The engravings in this remarkable work, though many of them possess great charm that may derive much from the French engravers, far exceed in their lack of accuracy Piranesi's departures from the truth which had aroused the indignation of Tatham (see page 45).

The inspiration of Carlton House, the Brighton Pavilion and Southill was no doubt already spreading into other great houses, such as Colworth, as we have seen. Sheraton's *Dictionary* brought all the distinctive features of the new Grecian taste as well as of the French fashion to the notice of an enormous public of cabinet-makers and their patrons.

For example we see illustrated in this work for the first time in England the

---

[1] *Library of the Fine Arts*, Vol. II, 1831, and *The Times Literary Supplement*, 31 July 1953.

Grecian couch with scrolled ends and lion-paw feet. Both principal types are shown, the sofa with ends of similar height and design and a stuffed back, and also the couch with one low end and a short scrolled arm. In his description of the plates Sheraton speaks of having seen some of the latest French chairs, which 'follow the antique taste and introduce into their arms and legs various heads of animals'. From this moment animal motifs are increasingly found in furniture, especially lion-masks and lion-heads used as capitals of legs, as well as lion-paw feet, and the animal monopodium shown by Sheraton as a winged chimera, with head, torso and single leg in one piece, forming one of the supports of a table. Lion-paw feet as designed by Sheraton were naturalistically formed (Plate 7); in the later Regency they were much more stylized (Plate 29).

An important feature now appearing is the inward curving leg for chairs of the kind that later evolved into the more refined form known as the scimitar-leg or sabre-leg. Here it is shown in the earlier form, of square section and with flat side-rails (Plate 39A), that appears in the hall seats supplied by Elward, Marsh and Tatham to the Brighton Pavilion in 1802, probably for the first time in England (Plate 2B). Sheraton also shows more delicate curved chair legs, but these are turned, in a manner developed from the turned and splayed out legs of his earlier designs, or they are fluted in a delicate manner reminiscent of the Louis Seize mode.

One of the most delightful themes in the Regency repertoire is that of the turned leg, with raised rings representing joints of bamboo (Plate 78A), and Sheraton shows them as legs for 'Supper Canterburies' and for the set of 'quartetto tables' (Plate 9A) or occasional tables on small splayed feet, that are among the most useful and popular articles of the period. They have affinities with the imitation bamboo furniture of a little earlier, and with the bamboo motifs seen in chairs which Georges Jacob supplied for the *Pavillon Chinois* of the Princesse de Kinsky.[1] The legs of the quartetto tables correspond closely with those of *guéridons* made by Georges Jacob and Weisweiler.

A characteristic feature now illustrated, often supposed to belong to a much later phase, is the splayed leg with a scroll-shaped knee, and ending with a brass lion-paw foot (Plates 59, 63, 65) used frequently for sofa and writing-tables. The delicate colonnettes which are formed at the angles of a secretary-bookcase and of cabinets and sideboards in these illustrations (Plate 56) also belong to the Louis Seize phase of design, but persisted for many years after in more thickened form. Other distinctive Louis Seize features that are prominent in later English Regency

[1] Ledoux-Lebard, *Les ébénistes parisiens, 1795 à 1830*, 1951, p. 138. See Note 8 (p. 147).

furniture are the columnar supports for cabinets, or table-legs in which the upper part is carried over the frieze, and the top of the cabinet or table is shaped outwards in the front or at the angles in a half-circle or three-quarters of a circle to cover it (Plates 50A, 51). In such instances the top of the leg or column is ribbed or turned in bobbin-like fashion (Plate 103) or fluted, often with concave sides (Plates 48, 49, 51). It is one of the most delightful features in the work of Benemann, Weisweiler, Molitor and Oeben, and appears in numerous articles of furniture throughout the Regency.

The aspiration towards the antique was expressed by Sheraton's giving some of his chairs the title of Herculaniums, and one of these possesses arms ending in small scrolls on concave supports sweeping down in a strong curve to the forelegs (which are decorated in this case with female heads). This is a theme used earlier by Georges Jacob about 1780, and again in the Pavilion hall seats (Plate 2B), but the book still shows also chair-arms curving down on to vertical arm-stumps in the manner of several years before.

Other chairs have crossing double-curved supports, paired back and front, sometimes of circular section, sometimes square. There is a design for a Pembroke table also with similar slender supports, of square section, and reeded like those of the chairs, that expresses one of the loveliest types of the Regency period in furniture (Plates 9B, 76B). This delightful theme, of classical origin, was used with extreme grace by the French *ébéniste* Benemann and in his favourite form with round tapering legs it was widely adopted throughout the Regency period (Plate 6).

It was at this time that motifs of dolphin and eagle, of late Roman origin and popular nearly a hundred years earlier in the designs of William Kent, as well as in French furniture of the Louis Quatorze period, began to come into favour again, though now with more slenderness and delicacy and usually on a smaller scale than before (Plates 10, 11, 29, 66A, 94).

Some designs in the *Dictionary*, such as those for the 'Sisters' cylinder bookcase' and the eagle-back cross-framed chair seem positively perverse in their ugliness and we are led sadly to believe that the brilliant mind that so marvellously conceived the pure and elegant designs of his earlier years has at last been brought to infirmity by the privations which he and his family suffered.

The *Cabinet-Maker, Upholsterer and General Artist's Encyclopaedia* was Sheraton's last work, published in parts from 1804 to 1806, but only thirty of the projected one hundred and twenty-five parts ever appeared.

The work was intended to contain articles as irrelevant to cabinet-making as

Astronomy, Bees, Botany, and Canada, but apart from these curious proposals the critics were ready to pounce upon the failings of one who was already believed to be insane. Many of the designs indeed might seem to speak of a disordered mind, especially such fantasies as the chair with shaggy lion-legs and camels forming the back, and the canopy-bed with grotesque winged chimera supports. But on the whole many of these last designs are no less well proportioned than those in his early works. The corner washing-stands have the old refinement, though now showing more fashionable motifs of reeded columns and swept legs, and one of the plates represents finely an early form of the classic chair of the Regency, the Trafalgar chair, with curved legs and rounded knees, reeded side-rails, and broad curving Grecian back. Other chair designs are no less refined and graceful, like the one with legs turned with rings representing bamboo joints, and a lattice-work back. There is also a Gothic pier-table with clustered legs which have capitals of naturalistic flowers so exquisitely drawn as to have delighted Ruskin.

The extravagance of some of the wilder designs, especially for chairs, need not be accounted as lunacy: the 'Nelson's chairs' with their almost surrealistically extravagant combinations of dolphins, anchors and cordage must have been intended to serve for the popular celebrations of the Admiral's victories that were common at the time rather than as solemn tributes to the national hero, and it is probably from them that the rope-pattern mouldings for the backs of the Trafalgar chairs derived (Plate 39B). The more elaborate and dignified form of this fantastic commemorative taste is to be seen in the famous suite of Dolphin furniture in the Admiralty House, Whitehall. Made by William Collins,[1] it was presented in 1813 to Greenwich Hospital by the widow of Mr. John Fish of Kempton Park, in memory of Nelson. The furniture is elaborately carved with dolphins, acanthus, cornucopias and other ornament, and richly gilded (Plate 11). Less extravagant but no less allusive examples by other makers exploited to the full the aesthetic qualities of the marine motifs of shell and dolphin, as in the unusually beautiful sofa, carved with marine emblems, from the collection of Lady Birley (Plate 10).

A great deal of the importance of the *Encyclopaedia* lies in its being the first publication in England of designs in the Egyptian taste. Here they are seen in the elementary forms of terminal figures with sphinx heads and feet, or with these features forming the capitals and bases of pilasters on cabinets, desks or sideboards (Plates 7, 14B, 17, 71). The full range of motifs in this strange style was to be exploited by others, and will be more fully considered in a later chapter.

[1] See Note 9 (p. 147).

43

Even greater significance may rest in the fact that despite the disagreeable and even demented character of some of the designs, there are to be found in the *Encyclopaedia* a great many motifs that were eventually purified in their form and context, and which came to constitute characteristic details of many of the most admired articles of furniture of the Regency period up to about 1815 and in fact many years later. Indeed it may fairly be said that it is in the *Cabinet Dictionary* and the *Encyclopaedia* of Sheraton that the domestic style of the Regency, as distinct from its exotic and purely antiquarian aspects, lies chiefly embodied.

Fig. 1. The sewing party, by Henry Moses, 1823.

THOMAS HOPE AND
CLASSICAL PURITY

Early in the nineteenth century the classical taste, fed from a hundred different sources, and most recently by the drawings of Tatham, was beginning to make such an impression on the fashionable world that the time was ripe for something approaching a codification of classical design applied to furniture, that would be useful to connoisseurs.

This new approach is discernible in Tatham's critical attitude towards Piranesi, who had until then been one of the principal delineators of the decorative themes of antiquity in Rome — 'rejecting with disdain the constraints of minute observation,' Tatham wrote, 'he has sometimes sacrificed accuracy to what he conceived the richer productions of a more fertile and exuberant mind.'

The 'Apollo of the Arts' of the early nineteenth century who was to be to furniture what Lord Burlington had been to architecture a hundred years earlier, was another Maecenas, Thomas Hope, whose house in Duchess Street, London, and The Deepdene, Dorking, became museums of the classical addiction in a new phase of severity and archaeological correctness.

Thomas Hope, born about 1770, was the eldest of the three sons of John Hope of Amsterdam, one of a rich family of Dutch merchants and bankers. He must have developed an intense love for the arts during his boyhood which he spent surrounded by a remarkable collection of treasures in his father's magnificent house near Haarlem. He dedicated himself to architecture when very young, and spent eight years drawing architectural remains in Egypt, Greece, Sicily, Turkey, Syria, Spain and other countries. Drawings made in Italy and Germany were the basis of an architectural work that was not published until four years after his death in 1831, *An Historical Essay on Architecture*. Eventually he followed other members of his family to England, where they had fled upon the occupation of Holland by the French in 1794. In this country Thomas Hope devoted himself to literature, and to collecting ancient sculpture, vases, Dutch and Italian paintings and other works of art. In 1801 he bought for 4,500 guineas Sir William Hamilton's second collection of classical vases, busts, torsos and bronzes.[1]

Quite clearly Hope was deeply concerned with the condition of the arts and the trends of taste of his time, and endeavoured to become accepted as an authority by the publication of his various works on architecture and furniture. He was a member of the Royal Society and the Society of Antiquaries, Vice-President of the Society for the Encouragement of Arts, and in 1800 he was elected a member of the Society of Dilettanti. Four years later the opportunity came for him to influence the direction of the arts, when he was invited by Francis Annesley, the first master of Downing College, Cambridge, to deliver his opinion upon the suitability of James Wyatt's plans for the projected college buildings. Hope's report had the object of discrediting Wyatt's design, which was his customary free adaptation of Greek and Roman themes, and resulted in the adoption of an uncompromisingly correct Greek design by William Wilkins.

Hope's first house was in Duchess Street, Portland Place, London, which had been built by Robert Adam for General Robert Clark, who died in 1797.[2] To accommodate his collections, Hope altered and remodelled the house, which was substantially complete in 1804, although in 1820 he added a second picture gallery designed by himself to display the collection of Flemish and Dutch pictures which were the property of his brother Henry Philip Hope.[3] The rooms were planned by Hope as backgrounds for his collections of Egyptian, Greek and Roman antiquities, with furniture also designed by himself upon ancient models to be appropriate for each setting. These designs were published by Hope in 1807 under the title *Household Furniture and Interior Decoration*, the work by which he is to-day chiefly remembered, and which served for years as a canon of the purified Greek, Roman and Egyptian tastes.

In 1807 Hope bought The Deepdene, near Dorking in Surrey, from Sir Charles Merrick Burrell, son of the famous Sussex historian and antiquary, Sir William Burrell. It is commonly believed that all furniture existing to-day which appears to have been made to Hope's designs must have been at Deepdene, and in fact it has been repeatedly stated by various authorities that Hope's book was intended as 'a record of the work at Deepdene', but this can hardly have been the case, because at the time of the publication of the work (and the preparation of it must have been completed at least several months beforehand) Deepdene had been in

---

[1] See Note 10 (p. 147).　　　　　　　[2] See Note 11 (p. 147).
[3] Westmacott, *British Galleries of Painting and Sculpture*, 1824, p. 230.

his possession for only a year, and no important alterations were carried out there, except to the grounds, until 1819, when the architect William Atkinson began his work, which continued until 1826.

The plates in *Household Furniture* correspond exactly to the description of the house in Duchess Street, London, as given by C. M. Westmacott,[1] which forms the basis of the description of the London house in John Timbs's *Curiosities of London*, 1857,[2] which is now quoted. The pictures and sculpture mentioned, which also appear in Hope's plates, further confirm the identification of the rooms.

'The collection was formed at the celebrated mansion in Duchess-street Portland-place, in the decoration of which Mr. Hope, the author of Anastasius,[3] exemplified the classic principles illustrated in his large work on *Household Furniture and Internal Decorations*, 1805 [sic]. Thus the suite of apartments included the *Egyptian or Black Room* with ornaments from scrolls of papyrus and mummy-cases; the furniture and ornaments were pale yellow and bluish-green, relieved by masses of black and gold (Hope's plate 6) *The Star Room*: emblems of Night below: and above, Aurora visit-(Hope's plate 8) [Fig. 3]. *The Blue or Indian Room*, in costly Oriental style ing Cephalus on Mount Ida, by Flaxman; furniture, wreathed figures of the Hours (Hope's plate 7). *The Closet or Boudoir*, hung with tent-like drapery; the mantelpiece an Egyptian portico; Egyptian, Hindoo, and Chinese idols and curiosities (Hope's plate 10). *Picture Gallery*: Ionic columns, entablature, and pediment from the Temple of Erectheus at Athens; car of Apollo, classic tables, pedestals, &c (Hope's plate 2). In four separate apartments were arranged 200 Greek vases, including two copies of the Barberini or Portland Vase; the furniture partly from Pompeian models (Hope's plates 3, 4 & 5). *The New Gallery*, for 100 pictures of the Flemish school, antique bronzes and vases; furniture of elegant Grecian design. Mr. Hope died at Duchess-street in 1831; he will ever be remembered for his taste and munificence as the early patron of Chantrey, Flaxman, Canova, and Thorwaldsen.'

The public were admitted by 'application signed by some persons of known character and taste'.[4]

It would appear that the rooms at Deepdene, which were not completed till many years after the publication of *Household Furniture*, never served as back-grounds of the various antiquarian styles to the same extent as those in the Duchess Street house.

It was not until 1824 that Westmacott wrote:
'the fine collection of antique sculptures . . . are shortly to be removed to the

[1] Westmacott, p. 211.   [2] Timbs, p. 557.   [3] A best-selling classical romance.   [4] Westmacott.

liberal proprietor's beautiful seat at Deepdene, near Dorking, Surrey, where a new gallery and amphitheatre have been erected on purpose to receive them. The pictures and unique collection of vases will remain at present, as will also the Canova Venus.'[1] The Egyptian Room at Deepdene, which was not formed until many years later, was described as 'the only eccentric room in the house' and as 'decorated in a heavy Egyptian style, with a quantity of dull red paint'.[2]

However, eventually a number of pieces of furniture were transferred from Duchess Street to Deepdene, probably after 1824. They remained there with the other collections until as late as 1917, when they were dispersed by public auction. A list of the articles of furniture appearing in the plates of *Household Furniture* which were sold at Deepdene at this time appears as an appendix to this work.[3]

There were comparatively few pieces of classical and Egyptian character at Deepdene. They numbered only eight lots, with another eight lots of French Empire pieces. There were many more articles of French eighteenth-century furniture of all three reigns, including articles of *boulle*. The house was extensively altered in an Italianate style in the 1840's for Thomas Hope's son, Henry Thomas Hope, and even more drastic changes were made in the 1870's.

After the sale the building became an hotel: until 1966 it was in the possession of the British Transport Commission.

To carry out his ideas and designs, Hope employed amongst other craftsmen, the carver Frederick Bogaert, who like himself came from Holland. He may have been the Frederick Boeges who did work for the Prince of Wales in 1795. He was presumably dead when, in *The Cabinet-Maker's and Upholsterer's Guide* of 1828, George Smith referred to him as a carver who was 'equally happy in his designs for furniture and other branches of interior decoration'. Hope also acknowledges his dependence upon a French craftsman, Decaix, a 'bronzist'.

Hope derived his inspiration from a wide variety of sources. He refers to his friendship with the French architect Charles Percier, who with his colleague Pierre François Léonard Fontaine, crystallized the French Empire style in the work *Recueil de décorations intérieures*, first published in 1801 and re-issued in 1812. Hope also expresses his debt to another work of Percier, *Édifices de Rome moderne*, and to Didot's edition of Horace with engraved vignettes by Percier.

The spirit that Hope absorbed from this source was again that of the neo-classic style which had been current in France for more than ten years and which had already supplied an enlivening influence in the furniture associated with

---

[1] Westmacott.   [2] Law, *Book of the Beresford Hopes*, 1925.   [3] Note 12 (p. 147).

Holland and Sheraton. Fully formed before the Revolution, it was the style upon which the fashions of the French Empire were based, and through Hope, it was of profound importance in the development of that aspect of Regency furniture which came to be called 'English Empire'. Like the pioneers of the style, Georges Jacob and Molitor, he favoured large expanses of flat veneer (Plate 19), decorated only with small ornaments of gilt metal, or with sparse inlay of ebony, and cultivated the forms of the chimera and lion. Apart from the identifiable pieces of Hope's design which survive, his influence is seen in a number of English articles of the period about 1805 or earlier, in which the shapes are rectangular and plain, and the surfaces free of ornament, other than inlay of ebony in classical forms such as the honeysuckle and palmette, or lozenges as in the French furniture of the Directoire.

An influential friend of Hope's was the sculptor Flaxman, whose 'Aurora and Cephalus' stood in the curtained Grecian room at Duchess Street, shown in *Household Furniture*, Fig. 6, and something of the sculptor's cool Apollonian classicism appears in Hope's Grecian designs.

In his researches Hope drew upon the records and recollections of his own travels in the eastern Mediterranean, upon his own collection of Greek vases, and those in the British Museum which, like his own, had been acquired from Sir William Hamilton. Hamilton's own work, the *Antiquities*, in four volumes published at Naples in 1766, with its coloured reproductions of Greek and 'Etruscan' vases, was probably used by him, as it was by Flaxman, and many other neo-classic designers of the late eighteenth century and after. The drawings of Greek vases in the works of Tischbein, D'Hancarville and Passeri were also acknowledged by him as valuable, and he derived many of his principal motifs from sculptures and other antiquities in the great museums and private collections not only of Rome, Florence and Portici (where the finds from Herculaneum were housed at the time, before they were moved to Naples), but even of the Electoral Gallery at Dresden which he had visited and where, years earlier, before journeying to Rome, Winckelmann had sought the 'eternal outline of the genuine antique'. Those collections which Hope had not seen were known to him through engravings. He also found inspiration in the great fundamental publications of the neo-Classic movement from the mid-eighteenth century onwards, including those of Winckelmann, its originator, and of Piranesi, his great antagonist in the Greek-Roman controversy. He used the great English contributions, James Stuart's and Nicholas Revett's *Antiquities of Athens*, Chandler's *Ionian Antiquities*, Robert Wood's *Ruins of*

Palmyra and *Ruins of Balbec*, and Robert Adam's *Ruins at Spalatro*; he knew the important French works, Le Roy's *Monuments de la Grèce*, Denon's *Voyages dans la Basse et la Haute Egypte*, Norden's *Egypt*, and the *Recueil d'antiquités* of the Comte de Caylus, which was especially sound and rich in its representation of antiquities from Pompeii and Herculaneum.

These publications possessed varying degrees of reliability and accuracy, but Hope seems to have drawn from them with the precise and unerring taste of a sophisticated, fastidious and cultivated cosmopolitan mind, using at the same time as it were the strict judgement of a banker's instinct to preserve the inspiration of antiquity against debasement of its currency. He was not entirely successful in this particular regard, because we find him complaining in his book that cabinet-makers had directly imitated his furniture even before its publication, and that 'extravagant caricatures' had started up in every corner of the capital.

In his Preface Hope sums up not only the principles of combining utility and comfort with beauty, that were among the aspirations of the Regency age, but expresses the essential character of much of the best furniture of his time — 'that breadth and repose of surface, that distinction and contrast of outline, that opposi-tion of plain and enriched parts, that harmony and significance of accessories . . . which are calculated to afford to the eye and mind the most lively, most per-manent, and most unfailing enjoyment'.

Hope's activities were not lacking in immediate effect on the fashionable houses of his time even before his book was published. Describing the period of 1803, P. H. Clayden, in his *Early Life of Samuel Rogers* wrote:

'The bow windows of Rogers's new house looked over the Green Park. He was fitting it up with great care . . . and had designed the furniture himself, with the assistance of Hope's work on the subject. . . . The furniture and decoration fol-lowed the Greek models.'[1]

Though apparently very extravagant, Thomas Hope's interiors were infinitely more restrained than the over-decorated settings illustrated by Percier and Fontaine, and which were actually executed for prominent French personages. Furthermore, Hope's furniture has much greater refinement of line and simplicity of ornament than many of the articles designed for the French interiors, which exhibited strongly the decline of style during the Empire.

Despite the magnitude, the complexity and the perfection in the execution of Hope's achievement — a *tour de force* fully meriting the title of 'virtuoso' con-

[1] Clayden, p. 448.

ferred on him by his biographers — Hope's furniture and interior settings might seem to represent little more than a self-contained episode in the development of Regency furniture, an archaeological fantasy, albeit on an immense scale. Their significance lies in the fact that the furniture was actually made, and widely copied, and that by means of the forms and ornaments that he selected and drew, the purified spirit of antiquity, with its austere dignity of design, passed into the general output of furniture and decoration of his time.

Hope's work had the result of establishing firmly such types of furniture as the circular table with supports in the form of three chimera monopodia (Fig. 10) and more generally and more attractively, with a single pedestal support of concave three-sided form (Plate 13); tables with lyre-shaped supports between baluster legs, or with monopodia legs (Plate 4A); supports formed of pairs of caryatids (Plate 15B and Fig. 5); *torchères* or vase-stands shaped as Grecian or Roman tripods; cross-framed chairs and stools (Plates 14A, 15A) often of simple form with reeding, or with rams' heads as finials; and couches of severely classical form, with stiffly upright scrolled ends and outward-sweeping feet with leaf-ornament (Fig. 10).

The circular table with triple monopodia, the couches, the sideboard with simple tapering reeded legs, the cheval-glasses with pediments, acroters and console-supports, and the caryatid tables, showed strong French character (Plate 15B and Fig. 5). One of Hope's designs for an armchair with arc-back and winged lion front-legs and arm-supports is identical with a model by Georges Jacob. The happiest forms encouraged in English furniture by his influence, however, were probably the typical shapes of the chairs popular from about 1805 to 1815. In Hope's designs we find the arc-back chair first seen in Sheraton's *Cabinet Dictionary* of 1803, and Hope has the earliest English published design for the chair with rounded knees and curved side-rails, sweeping in a single curve from the scimitar-legs to the scrolling top of the back-rails. Other minor details of design and construction that passed into common use through Hope's designs were the scrolled consoles, like brackets, joining straight end-supports of a table (or a cradle, see figure on title-page) on flat bases.

Amongst Hope's favourite decorative motifs, the honeysuckle was already familiar, and the palm-leaf ornament which so closely resembles it; so also were the fir-cones and acanthus leaves that he used, but Hope gave them new precision of style. The winged female figures of Victory holding wreaths aloft, and with their dress stylistically wind-blown, were imitated directly from French sources and helped to establish the 'English Empire' element in Regency furniture. A classical device which Hope popularized in this country was the use of metal bolt-heads as ornament, like the bolts in a Grecian door. Indeed, Hope illustrated a pair of such doors, one with plain bolt-heads, the other having them star-shaped, and it was through these designs that the star became a typical Regency decorative symbol, used to emphasize the joints in furniture, forming the back-plate of door-knobs, or set in line as the decoration of a chair rail or frieze of a cabinet or table.

This use of bolt-heads seems to have originated in Jacob's furniture for David's studio. They appear in his painting the *Return of Brutus* and they are used in the gilt armchairs and sofas at Southill, probably about 1800 (Plates 3, 5). Studs in the form of small paterae with flower-shaped heads were similarly used, and also the Greek key-pattern either as a design filling a panel or as a running frieze. Ornament of incised lines or grooving frequently appeared as well, all of these motifs being much favoured in architecture at this time and earlier, in these first days of the Greek revival, by its leaders George Dance and Sir John Soane.

Another device of French origin, given currency in this country through Hope's influence, was the column divided into symmetrical halves with a double lotus-ornament in the centre (Plate 88A). This theme is related to the common Empire feature of flat supports with the two halves of vase-shaped outline, divided by a disc or ball. The more elaborate ornaments of Hope's furniture, such as the couchant Egyptian lions used on the arm-rests of an Egyptian sofa and the viscera-jars forming finials to the back of chairs, were themselves impressive minor works of art, being beautifully modelled in bronze (Plate 21 and Fig. 3). Had Hope's furniture not been supremely well-made it would be ridiculous and contemptible, as were indeed many of the poor imitations made by inferior crafts-men. The precision of Hope's designs called for great excellence of craftsmanship, and thus Hope's archaeological approach had beneficial results, just as in the case of the Greek revival in architecture the execution of the precise designs of anti-quity brought into being more exacting standards of workmanship. Yet in some ways his vein of pedantic archaeological accuracy was contrary to the spirit of his time, which was marked by vitality, informality and exuberance, and above all by a sense of romantic poetry.

One cannot help feeling a great deal of sympathy with the criticism of Hope's book expressed in the *Edinburgh Review* by Sydney Smith, who was conscious of the great revolution in romantic poetry brought about by Wordsworth and Coleridge, when he wrote, 'After having banished the heathen gods and their attributes pretty well from our poetry we are to introduce them habitually into our eating-rooms, nurseries and stair-cases.'[1]

At the same time Hope's standpoint was not merely one of historical nostalgia, seeking to revive ancient manners which had become superseded in modern life. The prevailing forms of Hope's creations, when followed by others, lent themselves admirably to execution by the new industrial methods that were then being developed, in the beginnings of the Industrial Revolution.

Following the principles of French classical design, the structures of his furniture were mostly composed of straight pieces of simply formed timber, either solid, painted or veneered; they did not require to be shaped by hand as did many articles of former times, nor did carving enter into the decoration of main members to the same extent. Decoration mostly consisted of metal ornaments applied to plain wood. Almost the only direct ornamentation of the structural woodwork was by means of reeding, which emphasized the lines of the furniture and gave elegance and grace to parts that would have appeared heavier without it. The wider approval of this treatment, which was found to lend itself admirably to factory methods, followed upon Hope's adoption of it.

Thus an episode in the design of furniture which might well appear to be merely an antiquarian curiosity, while based on the motifs of the past, is seen at the same time to be part of the movement that lead to a purification of style, and to the functionalism of the modern age.

[1] *Edinburgh Review*, July 1807, p. 478.

Fig. 2. Engraving after a drawing by Tatham of a marble table with console supports.

GEORGE SMITH
AND FASHIONABLE TASTE BEFORE 1811

With the work of Sheraton and Hope the themes and motifs of Regency furniture were completely defined, but even before the publication of *Household Furniture*, as Hope himself complained, many of his designs had passed into general circulation and had become 'widely imitated in the upholstery and cabinet trades'.

The absorption of the fully developed Regency style into general furniture practice is represented by *A Collection of Designs for Household Furniture and Interior Decoration*, published in 1808, by George Smith, a cabinet-maker and upholsterer, then of 15 Prince's Street, Cavendish Square, London.[1] Smith was probably a tradesman of some importance, for he describes himself as 'Upholder Extraordinary to His Royal Highness the Prince of Wales' but there is no record of any pieces that were actually supplied by him to the Prince.

The designs in this book embody many of Hope's themes, though in a far less disciplined and rarified form. They obviously owe much to the great collector-designer's inspiration, yet although Smith's volume was published a year after Hope's, his plates are dated from 1804 to 1807. Hope's London house was open to members of the public from time to time[2] and we may fairly assume that Smith had not failed to look at the interiors and furniture that must have been arousing comment in the artistic and fashionable world even before Hope's book was issued. Smith's title also strikes one as a distinct echo of Hope's, where the phrase 'Interior Decoration' is used for the first time in a publication on the subject. An important difference between the two is that Smith's volume contains a comprehensive range of designs for a wide variety of different articles for the whole of a domestic household, both of the richest and of the more ordinary kind, whereas Hope's illustrations were solely of furniture and appendages for formal apartments. Smith provided designs for a wide variety of articles of furniture of every sort that might be needed, including many different patterns of beds and bed-posts. A great

[1] See Note 13 (p. 147).   [2] Westmacott. See p. 47.

54

many of Smith's designs are in the Gothic manner (Plate 23), and some in the Chinese taste, neither of which were favoured by Hope. It may be that Smith deliberately aimed at satisfying the popular market, which would not have been touched by Hope's scholarly work.

Although usually lacking in refinement, and sometimes extravagant in conception, Smith's designs are mostly very practical, as is to be expected of a working cabinet-maker, and are of tremendous value to modern designers and craftsmen in restoring or reproducing Regency interiors and furnishings, provided that they are used with taste, descretion and restraint. The designs for 'Window Cornices and Drapery' and for 'Cabinet and Frame Mouldings', for example, and many other details of furniture and interiors are of great value in this connection. An influence which Smith chiefly derived from French sources such as Percier and Fontaine[1] or from Hope is the use of animal monopodia for tables (Plates 22A, 22B) and legs of chairs. Indeed Smith seems to have become quite obsessed by animal forms, even to the extent of using naturalistic human feet of blackamoors for small tables, so that one can conceive of the furniture moving about by its own volition! Smith's lion or chimera legs for his Library Table' and for various forms of 'Library Chairs' have a robust and realistic animal vitality, quite different from the French Empire designs for animal monopodia, which are much more abstract and stylized. An important feature which Smith seems to have developed is the claw foot with wings used for the foot of a table or cabinet (Plate 24B). It is a device which had appeared earlier, in the design for 'A Chinese Light' in Sheraton's *Cabinet Encyclopaedia*.

It is strange that the fashionable evolution of the chair towards the elegant classic Trafalgar model seems to have escaped Smith, but this was probably because his predilections were for rectilinear lines, rather than for the curves which made that type so elegant and distinguished. There are three or four designs which show something of the great refinement of Hope's chairs. These have backs both of the crozier and the arc pattern, and there are some of Roman curule shape, but he repeats the pseudo-Grecian method of Hope and of Georges Jacob of joining a horizontal arm to a vertical post, or to a figure of a sphinx or winged female as an arm-support, often with a straight front leg, giving an angular appearance.

Among the more satisfying and harmonious motifs used by Hope and adopted by Smith are the console supports, like pairs of scrolled brackets, used vertically,

[1] See Note 14 (p. 147).

usually in conjunction with honeysuckle ornament, as the end-supports of some hall-seats and a dressing-table. A dressing-table using this theme similar to one designed by Smith is in the Victoria and Albert Museum (Plate 91). In the Royal Pavilion collection there is a map-cabinet of similar form (Plate 77B). This kind of support was drawn by Tatham from a marble table in 'a chapel near Rome' (Fig. 2), and that great innovator of the Empire style, Georges Jacob, used it for one of the designs shown in Percier and Fontaine's work *Décorations intérieures* of 1812. Hope's adaptation of the theme for a table was probably the immediate source of Smith's inspiration. It is illuminating to compare the three versions of the form. Hope's (Fig. 6) is far superior to Percier and Fontaine's, and to Smith's for delicacy, refinement and dynamic quality of line (see also Plate 1).

Other important motifs adopted and perpetuated by Smith were the divided column with a central lotus-leaf ornament, and the Persic column which had a lotus capital and base of identical shape and size. He also used this feature with turned shafts divided by a ball, deriving from French models. He adopted the decoration of widely spaced bolt-heads, either plain or of quatrefoil shape on the sides and fronts of chairs, sofas and beds, much as Hope did, but stars more rarely on chairs (Plate 42A) and on the friezes of small tables. He used straight-sided legs, square in section, and sometimes tapering, for the fronts of cabinets, with classical heads as capitals, and plinth bases. These derive through Hope from Percier and Fontaine and familiar earlier sources, as do his tripod stands with slender crooked-leg supports.

The importance and value of Smith is that he provides a complete guide to the furnishing of houses both of the richest and also of slightly more modest pretensions; his designs standardized the Regency style up to that time, embodying all its characteristic motifs and forms derived from Hope, Sheraton, Henry Holland and the French designers and from the sources in antiquity that had inspired them.

His work may seem to be lacking in the refinement and austere dignity of Tatham and Hope, especially the designs based on animal forms or other striking antique motifs, but many of them are bold and vigorous, and possess elements of fantasy and playfulness, which were important aspects of Regency furniture design.

The Egyptian, Gothic and other outlandish aspects of Smith's work are discussed in the chapters devoted to those particular styles.

For several years after the publication of George Smith's *Household Furniture* in 1808 no innovations were introduced in furniture design. In fact no comprehensive volume of fresh furniture drawings appeared for twelve years, when Richard

Brown's *Rudiments of Drawing Cabinet and Upholstery Furniture* was published, followed by the work of the two Nicholsons in 1826 and by Smith's final volume in 1828. Apart from the inspiration of his first work, for a time cabinet-makers continued to absorb the various influences, both French and classical, of Sheraton's *Cabinet Dictionary* and *Encyclopaedia* in the domestic tradition, and of Tatham and Hope in the antiquarian phase (the latter chiefly through George Smith's eyes).

The trends of taste in these years are expressed to a considerable extent in the pages of Ackermann's *Repository of Arts, Literature, Commerce, Manufactures, Fashions, and Politics*, which appeared, usually monthly, from 1809 to 1828. In Regency times this periodical combined the functions of *Vogue*, *House and Garden*, and *Country Life* in our own day. Although written in the pompous and verbose style of the time, it approached its various subjects with a spirit of excitement and vitality which caused it to run successfully for nearly twenty years.

In each number one colour plate and a page of text or less was, with occasional lapses, devoted to 'Fashionable Furniture'. The coloured fashion-plates for ladies showing the furniture with which the models are posed are almost as enlightening in the matter of contemporary taste, and probably more reliable on account of the absence of any desire to call attention to mere novelty (Plate 1).

It was the policy of the *Repository* to make a feature of the products of a single cabinet-maker or manufacturing firm over a fairly long period. One of the most important firms mentioned over and over again, especially at the beginning of the series, is that of Morgan and Sanders, established in 1801. Referring to an engraving of their Ware-room at Catherine Street, Strand, London, in the issue for August 1809, the *Repository* described their stock as consisting of 'patent sofa-beds, chair-beds, brass screw four-posts and tent bedsteads, newly invented Imperial dining-tables, portable chairs, Trafalgar sideboard and dining-tables, Pitt's cabinet globe writing-table, and numberless other articles' . . . 'They have been honoured with the patronage of Their Majesties and several branches of the Royal Family . . . they particularly mention the late Lord Nelson, for whose seat at Merton they were executing a considerable order, at the moment when the memorable battle of Trafalgar deprived his country of one of her most brilliant ornaments. As a tribute of respect to the victorious hero, the proprietors were induced to give their manufactory the name of Trafalgar House. In the premises in which this extensive concern is conducted, formed of six houses united, are daily employed nearly one hundred mechanics, besides other necessary servants. . . . Above ten times as many are gaining a livelihood immediately in the employ of Morgan and Sanders in different parts of London and its environs.'

An interesting article that was probably made by Morgan and Sanders is an elaborate cellarette of mahogany, with classical inlay of ebony lines, gilt lion-paw feet and lion-mask ring-handles. Once the property of Lord Nelson, and of the period 1803–5, it is now in the National Maritime Museum.*

In the earlier numbers some of the designs were supplied by George Smith 'whose classic taste in this line', said the *Repository*, 'is evinced in his splendid work on furniture and decoration,' and he was probably also responsible for the following observations in one of these numbers:

'Holding the antique as a groundwork for taste, a much lighter style evinces itself in modern works of art than has prevailed for some time; for which we are greatly indebted to the Grecian school, and which in the space of a very few years, bids far to give this country the pre-eminence, not only in execution, but in design.' These remarks would seem to have had a prophetic significance in respect of developments that were before long to ensue in continuance of classical taste.

Fig. 3. Thomas Hope's Egyptian Room at Duchess Street, London.

THE EGYPTIAN TASTE

There is no doubt that the Egyptian revival, as a fashionable craze, developed in France as a result of the intense interest in Egypt aroused by Napoleon's Expedition to Egypt and Syria from 1798 to 1801. His military forces were then accompanied by savants, one hundred and sixty artists and archaeologists, who formed the 'Institut des Sciences et des Arts', amongst them being Vivant Denon whose book, the *Voyages dans la Basse et la Haute Egypte* became the classic work on the forms of Egyptian art, and did much to foster European interest in them.

However, an interest in Egyptian antiquities and in the decorative possibilities of Egyptian forms and motifs had existed many years before Bonaparte's 'Retour d'Egypte'. Egyptian motifs appeared during the Renaissance in the work of Ghiberti, Mantegna, Pinturicchio and Raphael, and offered inspiration to Baroque architects in Bernard de Montfaucon's *Antiquité expliquée* of 1719–24, and the *Historische Architektur* of Bernard Fischer von Erlach in 1721. Obelisks and pyramids are familiar in the work of Vanbrugh, and sphinxes were popular features of the gates, terraces and steps of country houses and gardens early in the eighteenth century, though more likely deriving from Roman than Egyptian sources. At the time of the excavation of Pompeii in 1748, a collection of Egyptian antiquities was installed in the Capitoline Museum at Rome. These objects, found in the ruins of Hadrian's Villa at Tivoli, were the souvenirs of the Roman emperor's Egyptian campaign.

It was not to be long before the Comte de Caylus was to bring Egyptian antiquities to the notice of all Europe when his *Recueil des antiquités* was published from 1752 onwards. Considerable portions of the seven large volumes of this work were devoted to Egyptian objects, which existed in the principal European museums and private collections of the day, including the French king's cabinet of antiquities.

Winckelmann, twelve years later, showed Egyptian art in his *Histoire de l'art chez les anciens*, and in the following year Piranesi, his opponent in the battle of the Greek and Roman styles, was decorating the English Coffee House in the Piazza di Spagna in Rome with Egyptian figures, animals, hieroglyphs, symbols, and landscape scenes. An etching in his *Diversi maniere d'adornari i camini* of 1769 shows the room, which must have caused Egyptian themes to become familiar to many hundreds of English artists and men of taste who frequented the place, among them John Robert Cozens, Ozias Humphries, Fuseli and William Pars, as we know from the *Memoirs* of Thomas Jones.[1] About the same time the painter Mengs decorated the ceiling of the Camera dei Papiri in the Vatican with Egyptian themes, and the British architects Nathaniel and George Dance the Younger and Sir John Soane made use of Egyptian motifs.

It was not until the days of Percier and Fontaine and Thomas Hope that the Egyptian taste came to be applied with archaeological exactitude. Because they had at first been found in association with Greek and 'Etruscan' antiquities, Egyptian motifs came to be used as though part of the Graeco-Etruscan repertoire, and thus they appear in Louis Seize furniture not in isolation, but combined with Pompeian and other neo-classic features from a variety of sources, as in the boudoir of Marie Antoinette at Fontainebleau.

In the furniture of the brothers Jacob, and other *ébénistes* of this epoch, Egyptian motifs were used with freedom and imagination, as with the winged female sphinxes that appeared forming or supporting the arms of chairs, although the true Egyptian sphinx was male and without wings. At Southill Egyptian elements appeared in the drawing-room fireplace which has female Egyptian terminal figures in niches of the jambs, and the candelabra which stand on it may have been designed *en suite*. Flanking the chimney-piece are a pair of small gilt pedestal side-tables that are among the most exquisite productions of the Regency age. The kingwood tops have a double-gallery of ormolu, and the pedestals rise out of a bulbous base of lotus design, on small lion-paw feet, with the extended scrolling that suggests a date of about 1811 to 1815 (Plate 4B). It was probably from Tatham's drawings that the inspiration derived for these tables, candelabra and chimney-piece.

Several years before Napoleon stood before the Pyramids Charles Heathcote Tatham was in Rome making drawings of the Egyptian antiquities that he found there, and, as we know from the letters to his master, Holland, which are preserved in the Victoria and Albert Museum, arranging for the purchase by Holland of bronze candelabra and other fittings embodying winged sphinxes, Egyptian mummies, slaves and other figures. His drawings of winged female sphinxes in the Vatican Museum and the Villa Borghese, his figures of the eagle-god Horus

<hr>

[1] Walpole Society, Vol. 32: 1946–8, 1951.

(which he called Osiris), the 'Canopic jars' in the Vatican Museum, the lions from the foot of the Capitol steps and, finest of all, the magnificent Egyptian lions from the Fontana dei Termini, Rome, he published later in his volume of *Architectural Ornament*. But these were an early manifestation of the more scholarly aspects of the Egyptian taste, which were to be developed by Hope in his *Household Furniture* of 1807.

Vivant Denon's *Voyages dans la Basse et la Haute Egypte* was published in London in 1802 and Henry Holland seems to have made use of the book for the Egyptian motifs in the furniture at Southill and elsewhere, for a copy is known to have been in his library.[1]

In England the Egyptian interest was given the impetus of a fashionable craze by Nelson's victory of the Nile. The more serious enthusiasm of people of taste was aroused through the influence of Denon's 'grand publication', as George Smith wrote of it in his 1828 volume of designs. 'The novelty displayed throughout these fine specimens of art calling to recollection so distant a portion of ancient history, gave rise and life to a taste for this description of embellishment,'[2] he commented.

Always eager to illustrate the latest vogue, Sheraton included Egyptian motifs in his *Cabinet Encyclopaedia* of 1804–6, and although there is no hint of scholarship in his handling of the style, these designs nevertheless form the first publication of the Egyptian taste in England, and may have inspired some of the minor and popular uses of these motifs.

The scholarly interpretation of the Egyptian style embodied in Hope's designs were, as mentioned, from Denon, and from his own drawings. He had visited Egypt himself at the age of eighteen in 1788, at an early moment in the history of the revival. The Egyptian or Black Room at his London house, described by Westmacott as 'a little Canopus',[3] is illustrated in *Household Furniture* (Fig. 3). It had the walls decorated with designs from papyri, and the ceiling from mummy cases. The 'Closet for Egyptian, Hindoo and Chinese Curiosities' (Plate 10 of *Household Furniture*) was a small tented room with a fireplace like an Egyptian portico.

The popular imagination conceived of Nelson at the Nile as surrounded by crocodiles, and it is surely this mood of gay allusive fantasy that caused the library of a house described in *Our Village* to be 'all covered with hieroglyphies and swarming with furniture crocodiles and Sphinxes'. A brass decoration in the form

[1] See Note 15 (p. 148).   [2] See Note 16 (p. 148).   [3] Westmacott.

of a crocodile appeared on each of a pair of cabinets (Plate 16B) which stood at Embley, once the home of Florence Nightingale;[1] a similar device is to be seen on a hanging cabinet in the Victoria and Albert Museum,* and on the centre-piece of the Dolphin furniture at the Admiralty House in Whitehall. Perhaps the most beautiful examples of the Egyptian taste, however, are the cross-framed stools with decoration of lotuses which are sometimes to be found (Plate 15A), and the decorative motifs inspired by Egypt such as the slender legs of occasional tables, reeded and bound in the centre with a lotus-bud ornament (Plate 88A), and the themes of lotus-flower, papyrus and palm which were already familiar in classical designs. Terminal-figure supports for cabinets shaped with Egyptian heads and feet were probably among the commonest usages of the vogue, and not the least delightful (Plates 14B, 71). Such ornaments as these, and the winged disc of the sun were often executed in ormolu of the highest quality (Plate 17).

The lotus-flower and leaf became a widely adopted decorative motif, much used for the feet of sofas. The example illustrated (Plate 18) stands between the realistically Egyptian articles of Hope (Plate 21) and the pieces in which Egyptian inspiration became completely absorbed into the general tradition. By 1812 the Egyptian vogue was not yet superseded. In the *Repository* for May a design for a library-table has sphinx monopodia supports, and two years later in the number for July, an Ottoman couch is illustrated, with Egyptian terminal figures at the ends. In 1820 Richard Brown was following Hope's precedent by advocating that in a large house the styles should not be mixed, but each room fitted up consistently in one of the fashionable styles, among which was the Egyptian, and in 1826 the Nicholsons included the style amongst the Greek, Roman and Gothic as one which was in vogue.

Two years later George Smith published his third volume of furniture designs in which he pre-figured the taste of the age of William IV and Queen Victoria. In the Preface Smith makes the reference to Denon already quoted, but makes no mention of Hope, other than to acknowledge 'many flattering testimonies' received from him. There is a short chapter on 'Egyptian Decoration', referring to a single plate for an interior in that style. After referring to Piranesi's design for the coffee-room at Rome, which his own design to some extent resembles, Smith states that he has 'endeavoured to preserve the character of the Egyptian style without following its heaviness'. 'Under the hand of an intelligent and clever Artist', Smith went on, 'a room might be fitted up after this manner,

[1] Regency Exhibition Catalogue, 1952, No. 133.

possessing a light, yet imposing effect; although we are fully aware that this taste has been anathematized as barbarous, arising chiefly from the very injudicious manner in which it has been adopted.'

No other Egyptian designs appear in this significant volume of 1828. There are no Egyptian terms among the many designs for chair legs, no Egyptian sphinxes or heads in any of the furniture. All has been overgrown by the proliferating foliage of the Louis Quatorze, Rococo and Gothic revivals.

Fig. 4. The tea-party, by Henry Moses, 1823.

THE CHINESE TASTE

When the Chinese Room was made for the Prince of Wales at Carlton House, the Chinese taste had been well established in fashionable favour for over a hundred years.

The vogue had been in its heyday in the middle of the eighteenth century, when the numerous Chinese designs in Chippendale's *Gentleman and Cabinet-Maker's Director* reflected the interest in this fashion that was an offshoot of the Rococo taste, providing gay and delicate relief from the cold and pompous splendours of the Palladian style. In the second half of the century the taste was declining, although, as at Harewood* and Nostell Priory* in Yorkshire, Robert Adam was covering the walls of smaller rooms with Chinese wallpapers, and Thomas Chippendale was making about 1770 for the latter house those commodes of green Chinese lacquer that are amongst the loveliest of his creations.

All through the century the vogue never entirely died out, and the Prince's Chinese Room at Carlton House was part of at least a Royal revival of the taste that had been signalized by the building of the Pagoda in the gardens of Kew Palace for Augusta, Princess Dowager of Wales, to the design of Sir William Chambers. This Swedish-born architect who had made a voyage to China in his youth published his volume *Designs of Chinese Buildings*, *Furniture*, *Dresses*, *etc.* in 1757, and the Chinese Room seems to have been planned on the same lines as one of the interiors there shown. The furniture chiefly consisted of the two pairs of pier-tables and the arm-chairs, all of French Louis Seize character, already referred to.[1]

The Prince's next essay in the Chinese style was the transformation in this manner of the neo-classic interiors of the Brighton Pavilion* about the time that he renewed his association with Mrs. Fitzherbert. The 'Marine Pavilion' had been built in the form of a small but elegant villa by Henry Holland in 1787, in the restrained classical style that he christened 'Graeco-Roman'. The interior decoration had at first been in Holland's simplified version of the Adam manner, but by 1802, when the building was enlarged, the Prince seems to have tired of this

[1] See p. 30.

C. Furniture in 'the Chinese Taste' in the Corridor of the Royal Pavilion, Brighton. Chinese export bamboo chairs, cabinets of lacquer and simulated bamboo, c. 1802, and a drawing-room table, c. 1815.

chaste interior and wished for a gay and lively scheme of decoration that would be more appropriate for a seaside holiday palace.[1] The Prince is said to have been given some Chinese wallpapers, and he purchased through the firm of Crace and Sons enormous quantities of Chinese furniture, porcelain and curiosities of many kinds, from cargoes brought to England by Doctor James Garrett.[2]

It was thus that a Chinese style of decoration was adopted for the whole of the interior, and the Chinese Room which the Prince had formed at Carlton House nine years before was drawn upon to assist in creating the Chinese atmosphere at Brighton. In this first phase of the Chinese taste at Brighton the furniture, apart from the side-tables and chairs from Carlton House, consisted chiefly of the Chinese tables, chairs, 'sophas' and other articles made of bamboo for the European market at the end of the eighteenth century (Plate 24A).

The type had changed little since it was illustrated in Chambers's *Designs* in 1757. Such furniture also became very popular amongst some of the Prince's friends, who bought it for their houses, as did the 4th Earl Poulett for his Long Gallery at Hinton St. George, Somerset, which was entirely furnished with over one hundred chairs, sofas and tables of this kind. Other and rather more important articles of furniture, inspired in style by the Chinese export pieces, were supplied to the Pavilion in 1802 and thereabouts by the firm of Elward, Marsh and Tatham (Plate 24A).[3] While retaining the gaiety of the real Chinese articles, furniture of this kind, made in beech and painted yellow to represent bamboo supplied a satisfying element of English durability and stability (Plates 44, 45A, 45B).

The Chinese taste had always been especially indulged in bedrooms, and the articles of simulated bamboo became strongly favoured for such purposes in many English houses, as at Southill and at Uppark, Sussex,* where they were bought by the Prince's friend Sir Harry Fetherstonhaugh, while a fine suite of the same type was also collected at Dorneywood* in more recent years by the late Lord Courtauld-Thomson (Plate 27).

Amongst the articles made for the Pavilion then were a number of cabinets, some with imitation marble tops and ormolu galleries, some with plain tops and door-panels of Japanese lacquer (Plate 24A). These cabinets, although simulating bamboo, are inspired in their shape and proportions by the French articles of the Louis Seize period, but in place of the customary small-scale ormolu decoration in the frieze of each cabinet, there is an ornament of delicate cane-work.

This type of furniture was the only important innovation that the Chinese taste

---

[1] See Note 17 (p. 148).   [2] Royal Archives. See also Musgrave.   [3] Royal Archives.

introduced into furniture during the Regency. The greater part of *chinoiserie* furniture was based on accepted forms, such as commodes, cabinets, bookcases and similar pieces, in which the Chinese spirit was expressed by the doors, panels, sides and other surfaces being lacquered or japanned, usually in black and gold rather than in the green and gold or red and gold of earlier years (Plate 25). In a number of instances oriental lacquer and English japanned square cabinets were rebuilt as long low dwarf cupboards by the addition of curved side-wings with shelves (Plate 24B). Chinese forms, especially the pagoda motif, were occasionally introduced into conventional types of furniture such as chairs and sofas (Plate 26).

A fascinating minor expression of the Chinese vogue was the use of Chinese characters (authentic or otherwise) as motifs for brass-inlay work in the early phases of that fashion, from about 1810 to 1815, when small separate forms were used (Plate 34A). In the later phases of brass-inlay there was a revival of the *chinoiserie* motifs of Bérain among other Louis Quatorze *boulle* designs.

In his volume of 1808, George Smith has two Chinese designs, the first being a plate for 'Cornices and Window Drapery' in the Chinese taste. The 1828 volume, however, makes no mention of the Chinese style, although the Egyptian has been retained, and also the well-accepted Greek, Etruscan, Roman and Gothic styles, together with the new vogue, the freshly revived taste of Louis Quatorze.

The subject of Lacquer and Japanning, so closely bound up with the Chinese taste, is more fully dealt with in the chapter on Processes and Materials.

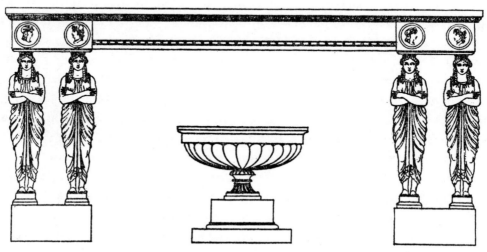

Fig. 5. Design by Thomas Hope for a table with caryatid supports. (See Plate 15G.)

THE FRENCH TASTE IN THE
LATER REGENCY

It is a remarkable fact that profound changes in the character of Regency furniture, amounting to the appearance of a completely different style, took place during the years of the constitutional Regency, between 1811 and 1820. The principal innovations were evident from about 1810 to 1815, and they had become more or less well established by the time of the Prince Regent's accession as King George IV.

The trends of design that were beginning to develop from 1810 onwards were of two principal kinds. One was to consist of a renewal of the pure classical influences of Tatham, Holland and Hope and eventually their absorption into the English tradition in an increasingly robust and homely insular fashion. Another significant movement of taste, brought about by the renewal of traffic with France following the fall of Napoleon, was the revival of interest in French styles, but less strongly now of the Louis Seize period, which was associated with the tragic events of the Revolution. There was a greater vogue for the styles of the late Empire and of the restoration that were favoured by the new French court.

This interest in French ideas was encouraged by the publication in Paris in 1812 of Percier and Fontaine's *Recueil des décorations intérieures*, which was now easily obtainable in England, and conveyed to the English mind the theatrical grandiloquence of the imperial palaces of Napoleon I, that was so different from the austere dignity of the early revolutionary style.

This fulsome Empire taste was acceptable to many fresh patrons of the decorative arts, especially amongst the industrialists and financiers who had been made newly wealthy by the Napoleonic Wars, and who lacked the discrimination and cultivated judgement of earlier patrons. During 1812, the year of Napoleon's reversal of fortune in Russia, the *Repository* illustrated designs of furniture in the French style in four successive numbers, and they continued to compete strongly with English designs for several years.

In 1814, after the abdication of Napoleon and the restoration of Louis XVIII, enormous numbers of English people revisited Paris. Relations between the two countries rapidly flourished and in February 1815, only a few days before the news of Napoleon's return from Elba, the *Repository* wrote:

'The interchange of feeling between this country and France, as it relates to matters of taste, has not been wholly suspended during the long and awful conflicts which have so greatly abridged the intercourse of the two nations, and as usual the taste of both has been improved.' In this number appeared designs for a French cottage bed 'as found in one of their country retreats', a French bed-chamber and a French sofa. Several designs in the heaviest French style appeared in the *Repository* for 1818, all obviously 'similar in design to those executed at Paris under the direction of Mons. Percier the architect'.

There followed a long stretch of several years when few furniture designs of any sort appeared in the *Repository*, most of the plates under the heading of 'Fashionable Furniture' being devoted to examples of window-drapery by John Stafford, the Bath upholsterer, and when at last the series was resumed one of the first to appear was again of French character, in the number for April 1822, for a secretaire-bookcase 'after the style so exquisitely perfected by M. Persée, the French architect to Buonparte'. Six months later the *Repository* remarked, apropos of a sofa, or French bed, 'The Taste for French furniture is carried to such an extent, that most elegantly furnished mansions, particularly in the sleeping rooms, are fitted up in French style.'

The *Repository* remarked upon the furniture made after French models by the firm of Snell in Albemarle Street, and it is possible that much Empire-looking English furniture came from this establishment.

An important factor affecting the trend of taste in aristocratic circles was undoubtedly the fondness of the Prince Regent for French furniture, which he had exercised since the first furnishing of Carlton House, and which he indulged even more strongly after his accession to the throne as King George IV, when he caused to be bought in Paris and in London magnificent examples of these articles, such as the many pieces he acquired at the sale at Christie's in 1823 of the George Watson Taylor Collection. In gratifying this taste for eighteenth-century French craftsmanship the King looked back to the golden days of the *ancien régime*, when the monarchy exercised exquisite judgement and taste in art. He seems never to have had any liking for the puritanically severe character of extreme neo-Greek design, which was generally associated with republican and radical notions.[1]

[1] See Note 18 (p. 148).

An interesting aspect of the King's taste for French furniture was a special liking for the art of inlay in tortoiseshell and brass practised by the Boulle family in the days of Louis XIV, and which played no small part in bringing about a revival in England of the decorative style of that period. It should not be forgotten that Louis Weltje, whom as cook and agent to the Prince of Wales, he had sent to Paris in his early years to buy French furniture, had married a grand-niece of A. C. Boulle, the cabinet-maker to Louis XIV.

Just before the Revolution the popularity of *boulle* had been revived amongst the French themselves. Work of Louis Quatorze design by later *ébénistes* such as Dubois[1] had been found difficult to distinguish from the earlier work, and Georges Jacob was called upon to execute and repair articles of *boulle* for the King. Indeed it may be said that Louis Quatorze motifs never entirely died out during the whole of the eighteenth century, for the distinctive spirally fluted peg-top feet of Louis Seize *commodes* were of Louis Quatorze origin, and there was *boulle*-work incorporating the broken curves of that style in some of the articles made by Weisweiler which were bought by the Regent. There were several superb articles of *boulle* furniture at the Brighton Pavilion in its later phases, from 1820 to 1823, and there are to-day at Buckingham Palace and Windsor Castle a number of magnificent early French pieces from Carlton House and Brighton, inlaid with brass, ebony and tortoiseshell, some with designs in the style of the Louis Quatorze artist, Jean Berain. 'A capital mahogany pedestal library-table inlaid with Buhl bordering' which was supplied to the Prince in 1810 for the sum of £84 by George Oakley of 8 Old Bond Street,[2] must have been one of the earliest examples in this country of the reviving fashion. By 1815 the taste was sufficiently established for a Frenchman, Louis Le Gaigneur, to open a 'buhl factory' at 19 Queen Street, Edgware Road, London. The Royal Archives record the purchase by the Prince Regent of several articles from Le Gaigneur in 1815–16. A pair of writing-tables bearing his mark are at Windsor Castle and a similar one is in the Wallace Collection.[3] All are in strict Louis XIV style. Mr. Bryan Reade has suggested[4] that the Prince's friend, Beau Brummell, encouraged him in his love for these articles, before he left this country in 1816. 'As might be expected in an extreme narcissist, the Beau was haunted throughout his life by a craving for the unique, the nonpareil — a craving he partly fulfilled. . . . In the absolutist world of Louis XIV he saw himself, or wished to see himself, at home; and it seems likely that Brummell, as

[1] Dreyfus, *Le mobilier français*, 1921, Plate 28.   [2] Royal Archives.
[3] F. J. B. Watson, Catalogue of furniture in the Wallace Collection, p. 244.
[4] Bryan Reade, *Regency Antiques*, 1953.

arbiter elegantiarum of the Regency, helped to create the vogue for Louis Quatorze surroundings.'

Following the Royal precedent the collecting of *boulle* furniture became fashionable, and very soon 'English buhl' was being supplied to a wider circle of patrons from the workshops of Thomas Parker in Air Street, and of George Bullock at 4 Tenterden Street, Hanover Square. The latter used the French technique, as will be seen, to express English designs of native flowers and plants.

The establishment in fashionable favour of the Louis Quatorze style has sometimes been regarded as marked by the publication of a design in that manner in George Smith's volume of 1828 for the interior of Crockford's Club, a famous gaming-house in Piccadilly, which was redecorated in 1826. This establishment, however, was but one of the series of buildings remodelled in the revived French style by the same architects, Benjamin Dean Wyatt, the eldest son of James Wyatt, assisted by his youngest brother, Philip Wyatt.

The first house of the series was Belvoir Castle,* where the famous Elizabeth Saloon was formed for the 5th Duchess of Rutland in 1825, with the aid of panelling from a château said to have once belonged to Madame de Maintenon, mistress of Louis XIV.[1]

This creation was followed by other great houses, all with their interiors decorated in Louis Quatorze fashion by the same architects; York House (later Stafford House, now Lancaster House) in 1825–6; Londonderry House, 1825–8; and Apsley House* for the Duke of Wellington in 1828.

The Duke and Duchess of Rutland had been among the first English people to visit France after the temporary eclipse of Napoleon in 1814, and they presumably bought French furniture on that occasion, for the bedroom of the Duchess is furnished with French articles of exquisite quality, as are also the King's bed-room, dressing-room and sitting-room at Belvoir, which were used by George IV during a visit he made there. These purchases, and that of the Louis XIV panelling for the Elizabeth Saloon, were thus of far-reaching influence in the furtherance of French ideas for furnishing and decoration in this country.

The King's rooms at Belvoir contain as well some English pieces, including a magnificent state canopy-bed, and a sofa-bed with high ends and corner-posts of the type illustrated by Sheraton in his *Encyclopaedia* (Plate 92A). The walls of these rooms were hung with Chinese wall-papers, a pretty compliment to the King's oriental tastes.

[1] Eller, *History of Belvoir*, 1841. See also C. Hussey, in *Country Life*, 27 December 1956.

Although for a time *boulle* motifs of the late seventeenth and early eighteenth century were employed in the brass-inlay decorating furniture of typical current design, it was found more natural and logical to adopt Louis Quatorze forms and structural features, as well as *boulle* decoration, especially for such articles as dwarf cabinets and large commodes or *buffets*, which are strongly characteristic of late Regency forms. These were on plinths with solid fronts, or cut-out with a drooping apron-piece (Plate 36), and were often made of ebonized wood to represent the ebony used in the Louis Quatorze era, as in the example of the large dwarf cupboard at Uppark,* Sussex, bought about 1820 by Sir Harry Fetherston-haugh, a friend of the Prince Regent, which is of ebonized mahogany and has column supports with ivory capitals and bases. When the plinths were supported on feet these were often of the bun-shaped sort, sometimes with heavily ribbed gadrooned ornament, of the kind originating in Louis Quatorze days, but also appearing in French-inspired designs in Sheraton's *Dictionary* (Plate 92A), some of which were republished in 1812. If peg-top feet were used, they were heavily turned in the manner of their early origin. Gilt metal ornaments in the form of female masks, set sometimes in a surrounding shell-shaped motif, were extensively used, especially in door-panels and cabinet-friezes, and in the apron-piece of a plinth (Plate 36). Circular plaques of bronze modelled with classical scenes in relief now occasionally appeared in the same way that such plaques had been used in furniture made by A. C. Boulle and his contemporaries,[1] and occasionally panels of glass decorated with under-painting or in *verre-églomisé*[2] were used in a similar fashion.

Some impetus to the revival of Louis Quatorze features must have been given by the republication in 1812, six years after Sheraton's death, of a number of his designs from the *Cabinet Dictionary* of 1803, and the *Encyclopaedia* of 1804, in the volume entitled *Designs for Household Furniture*, obviously echoing the successful titles of Hope and Smith of five and four years earlier. Among these revived designs were not only those of the French sofa-bed (Plate 92A) with its Louis Quatorze bun-feet, but also the early eighteenth-century decorative theme (both French and English) of dolphins as supports for chairs and tables. The popularity of these motifs was probably greater in this later phase than when Sheraton first produced them, and their use at this time is seen in such magnificent examples as the Dolphin furniture of 1813 from Greenwich Hospital (Plate 11), the table of about

[1] Packer, *Paris Furniture by the Master Ébénists*, 1956, Fig. 5.
[2] See also p. 136.

1815 in the Royal Pavilion Collection (Plate 29), and the gilt shell-shaped seats with dolphin supports that are also there.

The popularity of these features was as long-lived as that of other motifs of the Louis Quatorze revival, for we find the *Repository* for May 1825, referring to a table with three dolphin supports that 'served without the aid of a stem'. Flat bases for the supports of small tables such as Pembroke, sofa- and writing-tables were also characteristic Louis Quatorze features that were now adopted, and heavily scrolled console supports for side-tables, sideboards and large writing-tables, having their upper parts ornamented with vigorous leaf-carving (Plate 33A).

In general, foliate ornament almost completely supplanted formal classical decorative motifs at this time, and all the foregoing features became distinctive marks of much furniture of the later Regency years, indeed well into Victorian times. These motifs and ornaments were eventually to be found not only in the furniture made for royal and aristocratic patrons, such as may be seen at Windsor and Belvoir, but in numerous well-proportioned articles made for middle-class houses. Approval of the new French vogue was, however, far from universal. In October 1828, the *Repository* observed: 'The design of a bed in the annexed plate is in the Grecian style . . . which it is to be hoped, for the honour of modern art, will eventually succeed the heavy, cumbrous, and we may almost add, unmeaning decoration of the style denominated that of Louis XIV.' In the general debasement of taste later in the nineteenth century, this fashion with its profuse ornament and use of showy materials, was one particularly susceptible to the inroads of vulgarity.

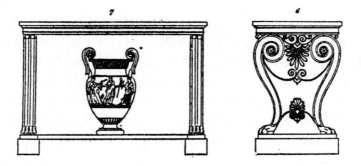

Fig. 6. Design by Thomas Hope for a table with console supports.

FASHIONABLE TASTE AFTER 1811

In the movements of style which took place during the years of the constitutional Regency, the principal rival to the growing ascendancy of French fashion was a renewal of the classical influences which had been formed by Tatham, Hope and Smith. After the death of Holland in 1806 the Prince of Wales made many changes at Carlton House, redressing it lavishly in crimson and gold under the influence of the amateur decorator and connoisseur Walsh Porter, greatly modifying thereby the severity of the 'chaste palace' which Horace Walpole had praised when it was first built.[1]

Apart from the French furniture of the *grand siècle* with which he encouraged the vogue for elaborate French styles, many of the articles bought by the Prince from then on reflected, and seem even to have precipitated some of the more florid and opulent tendencies in later Regency furniture. Such were the gilt settees made by Tatham and Bailey in 1810, their backs carved with shell ornament and broad-grooved scrolling in a manner later to become general. The gilt armchairs made by Morel and Hughes in 1812, with their outswept back-yokes, also anticipated later tendencies.

In the first years of this new phase, however, from about 1811 to 1815, the English furniture bought by the Prince still expressed something of Louis Seize and pre-revolutionary influences, and retained much of the purity of the early classical canons. Such influences survived in the very restrained gilt dining-chairs of Trafalgar type made for Carlton House in 1813. The magnificent pair of gilt council chairs, once at Carlton House (Plates 28A, 28B) are almost certainly the 'two very large antique elbow-chairs' made by Tatham and Bailey in 1813,[2] and are among the most superb creations of this middle phase of Regency taste. Obviously deriving from the classical designs of Charles Tatham, they mark the continued influence of these exemplars. Indeed, the publication of a new edition of these designs in 1810 not only must have given them continued force, but speaks also of the general demand for such models, probably among cabinet-makers no less than architects.

The national excitement at the beginning of the Regency coincided with mount-

---

[1] Walpole, Vol. 9, p. 14.   [2] Clifford Smith, p. 148.

ing successes in the war against Napoleon, and encouraged thoughts of creating new surroundings for life in the new era. Leadership in the world of taste lay much with the Prince Regent, even though it may not have been so in the world of politics. Southill was one of the houses where additions were being made at this time, so also was Hartwell, and the furniture for both of these came from the Prince's firm of cabinet-makers.

Some of the finest articles of furniture at Southill must belong to the years from 1808, when expenditure was at an average of nearly £1,000 a year until the death of Samuel Whitbread II in 1815. Judging by this level of expenditure some of the articles must have been important, as we may reckon among them, on stylistic grounds, the handsome circular drawing-room table (Plate 31) which displays characteristic marks of the later Regency in the rich leaf-carving of the base, and the light tone of the kingwood used. The small kingwood and gilt writing-table at Southill (Plate 30) with fluted frieze and lion-mask ring-handles like the foregoing table, also has the bases carved with the luxuriant leaf-decoration and spiralling tendrils of ornament that are distinctive of a great deal of later Regency furniture. The bold, almost baroque double-scrolled base of another large table at Southill (Plate 6) shows early signs of the returning vogue for the style of Louis Quatorze, but other decoration in all these pieces has close affinities with Charles Tatham's classical designs, which we may safely presume to have been among the major sources of inspiration for this firm. A wide circle of craftsmen must have been reached not only by Tatham's new edition, but by the publication of a new volume of designs by George Smith in 1812, entitled *A Collection of Ornamental Designs after the Manner of the Antique, for the use of Architects, Ornamental Painters, Statuaries, etc.* The probable significance of this work, published so soon after Tatham's new edition, should not be overlooked. The book consists of one of the finest collections of classical designs and ornaments that appeared at any time during the Regency, including many which seem to have derived from Tatham. They show, among numerous standard classical motifs, the elaborate florid scrollings and roaming tendrils such as are seen in Tatham, and which became so typical of later Regency classical ornament. Decorative motifs that are especially distinctive of this period, as well as the bold double-scrolls of table-bases already mentioned, are the small double-scroll devices with one scroll smaller than the other, and ornamented with a triangular bunch of honeysuckle petals or palm-leaves, or sometimes a shell or fan-like decoration tucked into the corners of the scrolls.

Although only one page of Smith's 1812 book is devoted to furniture designs, in fact four drawings for supports of sideboards, the work must have been influential, together with Tatham's book, in perpetuating fine standards of classical design during the mid-Regency years, and the two may have been responsible for much of the classical furniture that was produced between 1811 and 1815 (Plates 47A, 73). As well as the handsome library-table already mentioned a number of other magnificent pieces of the same period were included in the Hartwell sale of July 1938. Such pieces represent the middle phases of Regency taste in their finest form, displaying classicism in a rich and florid mood, but still retaining dignity and good proportion.

These qualities are finely seen in the remarkable mahogany and gilt furniture made for Stourhead* by the younger Chippendale in 1812. The armchairs[1] have a large and striking open *guilloche* ornament around the sides and backs, while the tapering, reeded legs look back to Chippendale's earlier inspiration from the French, but have taken on new sturdiness. The two open music-cabinets *en suite* with the chairs are most unusual, and possess similar masculine boldness.

The publication of Tatham's and Smith's volumes of designs at this time were not the only correctives then issued against unenlightened taste. Describing a Gothic sofa, table, chair and footstool in the *Repository* for June 1810, the commentator (who was probably George Smith himself) gave a warning that:

'no person of a genuine taste will introduce articles in this style into his apartments, unless there be a general correspondence in the appearance of his house. . . . By inattention to this principle, we have known individuals, of high reputation in matters of taste, absolutely fall into the grotesque and ridiculous. That was the character of the residence of the late Mr. Walsh Porter, at Fulham, no connoisseur will be bold enough to deny. It seemed to be the study of this gentleman's life to crowd together into so small a compass every diversity of style. . . . An apartment, decorated with all the gaudy fineries of China, led you into a cavern where you trembled lest you should encounter the dagger of some assassin; . . . you were ushered into a Turkish pavilion, which perhaps conducted you into a Gothic apartment, and that into a Grecian &c., &c.'

The very Gothic table that inspired this diatribe did in fact embody the anomaly of Tatham's classical console end-supports! However, there was a healthy urge towards consistency as a remedy against the more grotesque abuses of style.

The continued popularity of Tatham's motif of classical table-supports is shown

[1] Illustrated in Edwards *Dictionary*.

75

also in the *Repository* for January 1813, when the same type of article appears in a fashion plate for a lady's walking dress, obviously accurately drawn from a contemporary piece (Plate 1). The impact of the proclamation of the Regency in 1811 is reflected in a remark in the December issue for that year to the effect that the Prince of Wales's feathers continued to be used in the decoration of furniture as 'the Regent's plume of feathers'. The same number refers also to the maintained popularity of 'the fashionable Trafalgar chair, with a French stuffed cushion . . .'.

In the midst of these fluctuations of taste and style, no little influence may have exercized by the republication in 1812 of Sheraton's later designs in the volume *Designs for Household Furniture*, already mentioned. Fresh currency may have been given by this work to a number of early restrained designs and motifs, such as turned 'bamboo'-ringed chair and cabinet legs, Louis Seize colonettes, cross-framed writing-tables, as well as the French-type sofa-bed and the use of dolphin supports spoken of earlier. The more extravagant designs of Sheraton's later years also may have found more ready acceptance in a fashionable climate that was now becoming more tolerant of exuberance and elaboration. From this time onwards classical feeling in furniture design was expressed with differences that became more marked after the accession of the Regent as King George IV in 1820.

Profound psychological changes were no doubt at the root of the alterations in the mood of taste that took place from about 1811 onwards. The relaxation of tension from a state of wartime discipline and austerity into the more easy-going ways of peace; the prosperity brought to the middle classes by the war; the sense of triumph and grandeur prevailing in England after the fall of Napoleon, when London was the capital of allied Europe; the increasing indulgence of solid domestic virtues by the newly wealthy middle classes, in place of the cultivation of delicate aesthetic sensibility in the early years of the century by an informed aristocracy; all these influences may have favoured the new trends of design. Formal and abstract classical ornament gave place more and more to naturalistic leaf and flower decoration, and where such familiar classical motifs as the honeysuckle, lotus, palm-leaf and scroll-patterns were retained, they were formed in a more luxuriant and bold manner (Plate 37). The refined and even austere lines of earlier Regency furniture gave way to more massive and imposing proportions.

The more delicate types of furniture, such as sofa-tables with end-flaps and light supports were superseded by articles with tops in a single piece and with more solid pedestal supports, and by massive kinds of furniture such as imposing drawing-room tables on elaborate pedestals and bases, and large commodes and cabinets. This tendency towards heavier scale and proportion was to some extent mitigated by the use of woods of a lighter tone than were previously used, such as amboyna (Plates 29, 63), kingwood (Plate 31), thuya, pollarded oak (Plate 73) and elm, and once again after a long eclipse, satinwood (Plate 72), together with its popular substitute, maple. All these light woods were now in greater favour than the darker rosewood and mahogany of earlier years.

The greater use of British woods had been advocated by George Bullock, and was later supported by Richard Brown, his apologist. In the *Repository* also, for January 1824, it was observed, 'The manufacture of British woods such as the Pollard oak cut transversely near the roots, is now so well understood, and so beautiful when thus applied that they need no other recommendation to the admirer of superior furniture.'

The gleaming brass-inlay which had contrasted so richly with the darker woods was no longer so effective, and instead the 'bird's-eye' grain of the cross-cut woods (see page 141) was relied upon alone to give a splendid effect, or cast mouldings of ormolu were used, and inlays of dark woods such as yew to contrast with the lighter surface. This fashion led into the vogue during the 1830's and 40's for maple and satinwood furniture inlaid with holly in leaf designs, the edges of the inlay darkened by being dipped in hot sand.[1]

All these movements of style had become firmly established in the early 1820's, and found their expression in the works of Richard Brown, of Peter and Michael Angelo Nicholson, of Henry Whitaker, and in the final book of furniture designs of George Smith. In the midst of growing tendencies towards the overblown and the over-ornate, the first of these designer-authors pursued a purifying mission into the realm of decorative symbolism, with his *Rudiments of Drawing Cabinet and Upholstery Furniture*, published in 1820.

'Before the cabinet-makers were acquainted with the works of the Greek school, and had acquired a knowledge of drawing, their designs were made up of the most trivial conceits . . . their furniture was consequently quite void of taste . . . and labour was wasted upon transient whims of puerile fashion. But within these few years, their productions have assumed a new character, bold in the outline, rich and chaste in the ornaments, and durable from the rejection of little parts. This style, although in too many instances resembling the Grecian tombs, has evidently risen in a great measure from Mr. Hope's mythological work on House-hold Furniture, Mr. Smith's excellent book of Unique Designs, and Percier's

[1] Siddons, *The Cabinet-Maker's Guide*, 1830.

splendid French work on Interior Decoration. . . . Whatever ornaments are introduced into furniture should always be rich, graceful and consistent, and not of the vulgar kind: the quadrangular passion-flower, for instance, is extremely rich, the sun-flower vulgar, although we frequently see it introduced, with dolphins, darts, shells, and other incongruous appendages, on the poles of window-curtains. But the modern upholsterer and cabinet-maker now apparently try how disgusting and preposterous, as well as hideous, they can render their apartments, by the introduction of serpents and other reptiles, to which we have a natural antipathy.' In this summary fashion Brown dismissed the oriental fantasies of the Brighton Pavilion, which was being completed at the time his book was published.

For such articles as library furniture Brown considered appropriate such symbols as 'two genii striving for the bays', horned owls 'this bird being sacred to Minerva, and the lyre of Apollo, the god of Poetry and of the Muses, and likewise presiding over the sciences.' But he regarded no ornament more suitable for a library than the laurel 'an emblem of reward employed for twining about the brows of poets and others famed for science and erudition'. A loo-table, being used also to breakfast on, could have not only the tea-tree and coffee-plant for its ornaments, but also the masks of Ceres and Bacchus. This last apparently did not appear as incongruous to Brown in Regency times as it does to us nowadays. A writing-table might be decorated with the head of Mercury, the divine messenger, and his emblem the caduceus. If 'botanical enrichments' were desired, the papyrus plant was appropriate. The figure of Narcissus was suitable for a dressing-glass or daffodils and Narcissus-flowers. Masks of Bacchus were of course obvious choices for side-boards, together with vine-leaves and clustered grapes. For sofas the *gramen caninum* or couch-flower could be used (a nice example of symbolic punning) or the garden heartsease. The Graces with their attributes were fitting to adorn the dressing-table, or running fig-leaves 'to denote the dress of our first parents'. The Egyptian lotus provided the basis of design for a window-seat, or other flowers 'relative to rest and composure'. As well as the classical acanthus, honeysuckle and palm, the Egyptian lotus and papyrus, that were already familiar items in the antiquarian repertoire, Brown brings into his work a breath of the English country-side with the vernacular plants he considers suitable also for ornamental purposes, bergamot, jasmines, roses, lilies of the valley, running flowers of English hearts-ease, or pansy-violets — 'a low, trailing flower very delightful for its fragrance' — daffodils, Narcissus-flowers, columbines, a bunch of poppies, nightshade, hyacinth, and the night-flowering Cereus, a magnificent illustration of which appears among the engravings of Thornton's *Flora*, a work Brown recommended as a source of fresh ornament.

Brown has been much criticized for carrying too far his pursuit of purity in ornament, indeed almost to the point of mysticism, but it seems likely that in those days many people were well-informed on the subject of decorative symbolism, and that it was a part of the sense of poetry that infused much of the art of the Regency period. Also there were no doubt not a few furniture manufacturers who applied the newly fashionable repertoires of classical, Egyptian or Gothic ornament, with as little comprehension and taste as the themes and motifs of modernism have been made use of by inferior designers in our own time, and Brown's purist attitude was in this way a valuable corrective.

In another part of his book Brown devotes considerable space to the study of Geometry and Perspective, like Sheraton and Smith before him. He reminds us that it was Chippendale who first 'began to urge the necessity of cabinet-makers studying perspective drawing', observing that 'without some knowledge of the rules of this science, the cabinet-maker cannot make the design of his work intelligible, nor show, in a little compass, the whole effect of the piece he is about to execute', and he quotes the saying of his great predecessor that perspective ought to be studied 'inasmuch as it is the very soul and basis of his art'.

Although confessing his debt to Thomas Hope, Brown's designs have much less archaeological exactitude. The severe lines of the Grecian and early Empire style were vanishing by his day, and forms were becoming more flowing and relaxed. Monopodia were less archaic, and were given human female heads rather than those of lions or leopards. There was an increasing heaviness in the proportions of furniture; end-supports for tables became thicker, and instead of delicate shallow reeding had their edges decorated with narrow, deep grooving. Table supports were also formed of triple members, joined by a circular central boss to which was connected the turned stretcher. There was a noticeable increase in the amount of turned work, probably due to the improvements in lathes. The most beautiful turned work was done when lathes were more simple, in the days of Hepplewhite and Sheraton. When lathes improved, they tended to take charge of design, by making deep cutting difficult to restrain. Turned corner colonettes, with centre ornaments, were now of heavy proportions, and widely spaced from the body of the cabinet. Sofas had stumpy turned feet, and the sweeping scimitar legs of the Trafalgar chair increasingly gave place to turned legs. Tables and cabinets were given bun-shaped feet with heavy ribs of gadroon ornament (Plate 53), which are so distinctive of the later fashion, although of Louis XIV origin, and even had reappeared as early as 1803 in Sheraton's *Cabinet Dictionary* (Plate 92A).

Brown also shows chairs having the curved yoke with semi-circular ends, shaped or carved in volutes, which originated about 1812[1] (Plate 40). All these tendencies were appearing increasingly in furniture and were to form typical features of the 1830's and early Victorian days.

An important final section of Brown's work is entitled 'An Elucidation of the Principles of Drawing Ornaments, on seven plates', and illustrates with finely drawn examples the familiar motifs of Grecian decoration, with the rules for drawing them. The book concludes with a highly spirited drawing, finely engraved, illustrating the origin of the Corinthian capital. This capital, now reintroduced into the world of Regency furniture where since the days of Charles Tatham and Henry Holland the austere Doric and Tuscan forms had held sway, marks the growing trend towards richness and floridity in the later Regency years. One of the most interesting passages in Brown's book is one in which he pays tribute to a distinguished colleague, George Bullock, whose work in brass-inlay has already been mentioned.

The researches of Mr. Bryan Reade have resulted in clearing up some of the mystery of this at one time shadowy figure, whose designs appeared in the *Repository* from 1816 to 1824, and whose work is mentioned intriguingly in the letters of Maria Edgeworth. It appears that this many-sided person was important in business as a sculptor, marble mason, upholsterer and cabinet-maker in Liverpool, and came to London in 1813 or 1814, where from 4 Tenterden Street he supplied not only furniture and upholstery, but fireplaces of Mona marble from Anglesey, a material he had no doubt been accustomed to use as a marble mason in Liverpool.

The first mention of Bullock and of brass-inlay in the *Repository* is in the number for February 1816, which has a plate showing a 'Drawing-room Window-curtain and Cabinet'. The latter is described as 'designed for execution in our native woods, relieved by inlaid metal ornaments'. Other designs for fireplaces and interiors appeared later in that year. They were stolidly insular in character and represented the English cabinet-maker's native and even provincial mistrust of French styles which were appearing more and more frequently in the *Repository* at

[1] See also p. 94.

this time. This attitude of his is expressed in a design for an English bed in the number for November 1816, selected 'for the tasteful simplicity that pervades it . . .'. The lines of the drapery, as well as of the head and foot boards, are simple and straight, and the front posts are short with turned shafts and feet. The design is in clear contrast to those of late Empire styles, with high boat-like curved ends, heavy carved gilt cornucopias at the sides, and drooping folds of drapery, that the *Repository* was now illustrating (Plate 92B). September 1817, brought three designs from Bullock for fashionable chairs, all hideous and lacking in grace, and all with the turned legs that were to become increasingly common. After this there is silence until June 1824, when some designs for a drawing-room table, chairs and footstools are described as in the style of 'the late Mr. Bullock'. It appears that he died in 1818. It is thus that Richard Brown sums up his achievement:

'The late Mr. Bullock was the only person who ventured into a new path: though some of his designs were certainly too massy and ponderous, nevertheless grandeur cannot be obtained without it; such are the standards to his octagon tables. There was great novelty without absurdity, as well as a happy relief, in his ornaments: yet many of his articles were considerably overcharged with buhl; sometimes the buhl-work was sunk in brass, and on other occasions the counterpart was of the same wood as the furniture itself, and the whole surface presented a brazen front. . . . Most of his ornaments were selected from British plants, and his woods were of English growth, which were admirably well polished. He has shewn that we need not roam to foreign climes for beautiful ornaments, but that we have abundance of plants and flowers equal to the Grecian, which, if adopted, would be found as pleasing as the antique.'

Maria Edgeworth admired some 'fine tables of Mr. Bullock's making' which she saw in 'a modern dressing-room' at Aston Hall,* Birmingham, in 1820, 'one of wood from Brazil — Zebra wood, and no more to be had for love or money.'[1]

Bullock was also responsible for a great deal of work at Abbotsford,* the home of his friend Sir Walter Scott, where Bullock worked in conjunction with the architect William Atkinson in planning the interior decoration. He provided tables and chairs, and the fireplaces in the drawing-room and armoury, between the years 1816 to 1818. The dining-room furniture is of plain design, in oak, the table being an extending one of the 'Imperial' type with a framed top, and all ten pieces, table, sideboard and chairs have sturdy but simple turned legs.

The handsome drawing-room table (Plate 35) with its brass-inlay of flower and

---

[1] Edgeworth, *Life and Letters*, Vol. II, 1894, p. 276.

leaf designs, may well be one of Bullock's octagon tables which Brown so much admired.

Valuable contributions have been made to our knowledge of Bullock's furniture by Mr. Anthony Coleridge in several articles[1] in which he describes important furniture supplied by Bullock to some great Scottish houses, including a pair of inlaid larchwood cabinets and a pair of circular inlaid tables at Blair Castle, Perthshire; some tables at Scone Palace; and the dining-room furniture at Abbotsford. There is also a very fine octagonal inlaid drawing-room table at Kinross House. Bullock's work played an important part in the vogue for buhl furniture, even if it stood apart from those articles of the kind that embodied the typical broken curves, arabesques and *chinoiserie* motifs of the Louis Quatorze phase of the movement. But in combining the French technique of metal inlay with English designs it may perhaps be said that Bullock helped to bring about the fusion of French influence with the English furniture tradition.[2]

Similar trends of design to those expressed by Brown were more fully exploited in the *Practical Cabinet Maker, Upholsterer and Complete Decorator*, by Peter and Michael Angelo Nicholson, father and son. The plates are dated 1826 and 1827, so the book was presumably published in the latter year. The work was planned by Peter Nicholson (1765–1844) the Scottish mathematician and architect who built additions to the University and various houses in Glasgow, designed Castleton House and Corby Castle, near Carlisle, and laid out the new part of Ardrossan, in Ayrshire. He was the first to perceive that the volutes of Ionic capitals should form logarithmic spirals, and that Grecian mouldings were formed from ellipses instead of circles, as were the Roman mouldings.

Most of the plates in the *Practical Cabinet Maker* were drawn by Michael Angelo, the son. He was an architectural draughtsman who had been a pupil of John Foulston, the architect of early nineteenth century Plymouth. Many of Michael Angelo's designs have pleasing elegance and good proportion, especially such articles as the bed-steps, some of the chair designs, and the 'Library Bookcase'.

The fashionable richness and profusion of leaf-decoration is expressed in all the designs, and also the increased tendency towards carved ornament, especially in bed-posts, chair and sideboard legs. The early Grecian arc-back with squared ends, and the scroll or crozier-back for chairs are retained, but there are several designs for the later chair-yokes shaped with volutes, and with elaborately carved back-splats. The legs, though straight, either square or heavily reeded, are still slender,

[1] See Bibliography.   [2] See also p. 129.

but carry more heavy leaf-ornament, and in one case the long carved lambrequins, like hanging sheaths of scalloped drapery, that are eventually to become common. The current fondness for luxuriant leaf-ornament again inspires the strongly swirling curves of sofa-backs (Plate 32A), growing into deeply carved acanthus and honeysuckle motifs, which are also used as cresting for the backs of sideboards (Plate 32B), and for the centres of pediments on book-cases (Plate 69), cabinets, wardrobes, (Plate 33B) cheval-glasses and dressing-glasses (Plate 89A).

There is a much more extensive range of designs in Nicholson than in Brown, especially for such things as bed-posts, chair and sofa legs, and sideboard legs and rails. These, together with all the decorative ornaments, the orders and most of the furniture designs are signed by M. A. Nicholson, the son. At the end of the book is a group of unsigned plates, which may have come from a quite different source, for they are distinctly inferior to those of Michael Angelo. They are mostly for French beds, commodes, chairs, a settee, and bedroom furniture and are extremely ponderous, at once exhibiting the debasement of the Empire style and foreshadowing the clumsiness of the mid-Victorian years. They may have been included merely to make the book more completely representative of current fashion.

An important characteristic of late Regency design fully expressed in Nicholson is the vigorous outgrowth of ornament where sofa, chair and table legs meet the parts they support, and in the scrolled feet of breakfast-tables, often in the form of bunched leaves or spiralling tendrils, as well as of extended classical scrolling. These features are a florid development of similar ornaments that were seen some years earlier, about 1811–15, at Southill in a small writing-table and in the drawing-room tables there (Plates 30, 31), in the library-table at Hartwell (Plate 72), and in other pieces of the period (Plates 47A, 73). The chief value of the Nicholsons' work must have been that it provided an exemplar of fine design at a moment when style was in danger of becoming debased, and though a great change had taken place in the character of forms, the mid-Victorian collapse of design was prevented from occurring sooner than it might otherwise have done.

With the almost complete victory of naturalistic leaf-ornament and decorations in inlay of native English plants and flowers, over the abstract, geometrical and formal classical ornament of the earlier Regency years, and in the return to favour of British oak and elm in furniture-making, through the influence of Bullock and Brown, it would seem that designers had at last taken to heart the comments of Sydney Smith in the *Edinburgh Review* on Hope's classical designs, and that the gods and goddesses had been finally routed by the nature philosophy of Wordsworth and the romantic poets, that by now was so much more truly part of the spirit of the age than the escapist intellectual nostalgia for Rome and Hellas.

Similar characteristics of the new style as those shown by Brown and Nicholsons are found in a volume issued by Henry Whitaker in 1825, in which we see again the fashionable heavily foliate crestings and voluted chair-backs. He looks back to the earlier years of the century in his continued use of lion-headed console-supports, and lion monopodia, but the newly popular Louis Quatorze and Louis Quinze motifs are to be found also, in such designs as the wall brackets with their rococo scrollings.

Although the Rococo revival of the nineteenth century had its beginnings in the Regency, the full development of this style with its flowing curves of chair legs and scroll feet was not attained until nearer the mid-century.

John Taylor, who contributed a number of designs to the *Repository* during the 1820's, published two small notebooks of furniture and drapery designs about 1825–6 with the title of *Upholsterer's and Cabinet Maker's Pocket Assistant*. It seems to have been intended as a popular guide to the standard types of furniture which remained most constantly in favour, which is perhaps why we find in it not only designs of the later pattern of sideboards and sofas, with bold crestings, but such early classical themes as Thomas Hope's circular table on a triangular pedestal in almost its original purity, and Tatham's pervasive design of console table-supports now applied to the pedestals of a sideboard. There are as well indications that bun-shaped feet and heavily-formed peg-top feet were rapidly displacing lion-paw feet for cabinets and tables.

The most important embodiment of the later phases of Regency taste is George Smith's last volume of designs, *The Cabinet-Maker's and Upholsterer's Guide*, which he produced after 'an experience of forty years' in the cabinet-making trade. As indicated on the letterpress title-page, it was published in 1828, although the decorative engraved title-page is dated 1826. The furniture plates date from 1826, most of the designs for interior decoration being of 1828.

In addition to the customary chapters on Geometry and Perspective there is an important section on Ornamental Drawing, showing numerous fine examples of ornaments, mostly in the current richly foliate manner.

An important development in later Regency furniture that is expressed in many of Smith's designs for wardrobes, commodes, bookcases and sideboards, as in numerous other contemporary designs for such objects, is the Egyptian and also Grecian theme of a depressed centre-portion between high wings (Plate 33B). This feature had an architectural parallel in Southgate Grove, Middlesex (1797) and in some of the villas of Regent's Park that were designed in this form by John Nash, following the principle of breaking up the masses of a structure, which was one of the cardinal tenets of the cult of the Picturesque. and had appeared also in a design for a writing-desk in Hope's book (Plate 19). Smith's later furniture designs in general lack the elegance of Nicholson's, with their gracefully proportioned shafts for bed-posts or cabinet and table-legs, and delicate leaf capitals and bases. Smith's are far more crude, the shafts being divided into several portions, each with a different (and often unrelated) variety of heavy turned or ribbed ornaments and leaf-shaped cups separating the different sections. The chair designs have completely lost the grace of earlier years. The front legs are straight, usually turned and heavily proportioned. There is an extravagantly carved French chair, in advanced Rococo taste with C-scrolls and shell-work, and an 'Indian Chair', which Smith possibly believed might commend itself to the King for the Brighton Pavilion. In chair-backs the development of the yoke with end-volutes to one with outward turned scrolling ends,[1] is now well-established, and chair-legs, like bed-posts, are divided into sections marked by cup-shaped leaf ornaments. In accordance with French post-Empire influences, Smith shows the bases of cabinets, washing-stands, dressing-tables, chests and many other articles shaped as platforms, and the tendency is now for them to be thick, plain and slab-shaped, often with rounded corners, and the feet are more commonly bun-shaped.

For drawing-room tables, cabinets, commodes and foot-stools Smith now shows lion-paw feet and feet of scroll form, both with the currently fashionable outgrowth of boldly formed leaf-ornament or spiral scrolling of leaves and honeysuckle. His designs for wardrobes and chimney-glasses have the heavily ornamented pediments that are also characteristic of the 1820's (Plates 32B, 33B), although they had appeared much earlier, in his volume of 1808. Despite these tendencies, many of the later designs by Smith are well-proportioned, especially for such articles as the drawing-room commodes and dwarf bookcases, and the pedestal 'candelabri'. Furthermore the almost complete absence of animal motifs in this late phase frees his work from the element of the grotesque that made his earlier designs distasteful to many patrons and connoisseurs.

[1] See also p. 94.

THE GOTHIC STYLE

The Gothic taste, that enjoyed so lively a popularity in the days of Chippendale, following Horace Walpole's adoption of the style at Strawberry Hill, receded from favour during the time of Adam and Hepplewhite, and there is no mention of it in Sheraton's first book. In the *Cabinet Dictionary*, however, Gothic detail appears once more, somewhat tentatively, in the canopy of a buffet and in a library bookcase. In the *Cabinet Encyclopaedia* a year later there are fully developed Gothic designs for two pier-tables, one of which has exquisitely drawn trailing ivy ornament, and delicate tracery with all the grace and playfulness that makes neo-Gothic detail so delightful at its best. There are also a bookcase and a bed with Gothic ornament, but of a heavier character.

Four years later George Smith provides a number of Gothic designs in his *Household Furniture*. One of his most elaborate state beds is in this style, which he chose as 'admitting of a more abundant variety of ornaments and forms that can possibly be obtained in any other style: and as many mansions of our Nobility and Gentry are at this time finished in a similar taste, this Design may not be deemed inacceptable'. There are designs in the Gothic style also for chairs, dumb-waiters, for large library bookcases and a delightful small bookcase with a drawer in the base (Plate 23). The library was one of the principal preserves of the Gothic taste, which so admirably encouraged visions of monastic study and meditation.

The *Repository's* commentator (who, as we shall see, was probably Augustus Pugin) wrote in March 1827, 'No style can be better adapted for its decoration (the Library) than that of the middle ages, which possesses a sedate and grave character, that invites the mind to study and reflection. The rays passing through its variegated casements cast a religious light upon the valuable tomes on either side, the beautiful arrangement of its parts combining to produce an impressive grandeur in the whole design.'

A few years earlier, in July 1813, the *Repository* was advocating late Gothic design for the movables of small picturesque houses: 'The cottage chair is composed after designs which prevailed in the sixteenth century . . . analogous to the purposes of a *cottage ornée*.'

Not only was Gothic furniture in keeping with the picturesque qualities of the rural architecture of Papworth and P. F. Robinson, who re-introduced the Tudor style in the Regency, it was an essential part of the mediaeval vision that was conjured up in the mind by the horrific Gothic novels of the day and the historical romances of Walter Scott, and that was brought into being in the gracefully and elegantly detailed Gothic creations of James Wyatt like Ashridge and Lee Priory; more ponderously in the immense mediaeval castles such as Lowther Castle and Eastnor Castle* in the 'square style' of Sir Robert Smirke.

A long series of exclusively Gothic designs began in the *Repository* in October 1825, with one for a bookcase in which the arches were made flat, 'which form is considered more appropriate for domestic architecture than the pointed, which seems better calculated for ecclesiastical purposes.'

At length the *Repository* was able to comment, in the number for August 1827, 'we have now so many skilful workers in Gothic, that very elaborate pieces of furniture may be made at a moderate price, compared with what it was a few years ago,' and again, in October of the same year: 'The Gothic style, which we have shown to be so well adapted to domestic arrangements and decorations, is becoming much more general than it was a few years since.'

While these Gothic fantasies were being produced, the furniture appearing incidentally in the ladies fashion plates of the *Repository* over this period were all obstinately classical.

In October 1827, the significance of the long series of mediaeval designs became apparent, when a plate was shown representing all the pieces which had been described assembled in a Gothic interior, with the announcement that the designs and their descriptions were shortly to be published separately under the title of Pugin's *Gothic Furniture*. It was issued in 1828. The artist thus revealed was Augustus Charles Pugin (1762–1832), John Nash's principal draughtsman, who was responsible for most of the Gothic detail in his master's work. Furniture designed by him, especially chairs of rosewood and gilt, with Gothic tracery backs, may be seen in the State Apartments at Windsor Castle.*

In the third decade of the nineteenth century interest in Gothic domestic architecture settled into a fondness chiefly for the simple flat-arched style of the sixteenth century, that was then being adopted extensively for villas, cottages and farm-houses, and the furniture intended to accord with these surroundings was of a simple sturdy Gothic rectilinear character (Plate 82).

While there may have been some dabblings in the Gothic style in the attempt to create the mediaeval world of Monk Lewis or Walter Scott, Gothic furniture was probably most sought after for its playful gaiety, especially when this kind of design was confined to elegant pointed tracery in chair-backs and bookcase ends rather than pursuing historical motifs to their extreme. This Pugin himself seems to have sensed when he commented in the *Repository* for March 1827, 'It has been generally considered that the architecture of the middle ages possesses more playfulness in its outline, and richness in its details, than any other style.'

It was the younger Pugin who substituted a mediaeval religious and didactic fervour in domestic design, as in ecclesiastical architecture, for a more delicately poetical vision of the ancient world, whether classical or Gothic, that prevailed in the Regency. He is probably even more famous than his father, because of his influence in the later phases of the Gothic revival, in which his book *Furniture in the Style of the Fifteenth Century*, published in 1835, had some importance. But the designs of the son had little of the fluid delicacy of the elder Pugin's adaptations of tracery to English furniture design, and appear hard and unsympathetic by contrast.

Fig. 7. Fireside conversation, by Henry Moses, 1823.

LOUDON AND
THE VICTORIAN THRESHOLD

The last phases of Regency furniture must not be imagined as a headlong descent into an abyss of crude and tasteless design. The charm of a great deal of early Victorian furniture testifies to the contrary. Michael Angelo Nicholson's fine and elegant drawings must have been not only a restraining, but a positively inspiring influence.

Another work was even more far-reaching in its effects amongst many different classes of the community, and confirmed the classical doctrines, which had been enunciated earlier in the fullest purity by Thomas Hope, as the enlivening and controlling spirit in vernacular furniture. This work was J. C. Loudon's *Encyclopaedia of Cottage, Farm and Villa Architecture and Furniture, containing numerous designs for dwellings from the cottage to the villa . . . with the requisite fittings-up, fixtures and furniture. . . .*

This remarkable volume, which extended to over 1300 pages, gave details of the furnishing not only of the best rooms of Villas, some of considerable size, but of the servants' rooms and other modest rooms in these and in the smallest houses and cottages. It was first published in 1833, and ran into several editions later. It presents a complete picture of the architecture and furnishing of many different kinds of house other than the very grand ones, as they were three years after the death of King George IV, revealing incidentally much of what everyday life was like in villas, farmhouses, inns and cottages. It is one of the most valuable social documents of its time.

There are designs for every conceivable grade and style of furniture and interior decoration and fitting, from the most elaborate Gothic four-poster bed, with many admirable designs for bed-posts, to the humblest servant's 'stump bedstead' of ironwork, or the folding press bedstead, 'very common in Kitchens', down to a child's go-cart, for teaching it to walk.

Discussing the furniture of villas, Loudon wrote: 'The principal Styles of Design in Furniture, as at present executed in Britain, may be reduced to four, viz., the Grecian or Modern style, which is by far the most prevalent; the Gothic or perpendicular style, which imitates the lines and angles of the Tudor Gothic Architecture; the Elizabethan, which combines the Gothic with the Roman or Italian manner; and the style of the age of Louis XIV., or the florid Italian, which is characterised by curved lines and excess of curvilinear ornaments. . . . We have given but few designs in the style of Louis XIV on account of the great expense of carrying them into execution.'

The designs for Grecian or modern furniture were made 'almost entirely by Mr. Dalziel, and indeed have been executed in his manufactory', but Loudon was not altogether satisfied with his drawings, for he did not hesitate to criticize them for their faults of style and design. Writing of a chair, for example, he asks, 'Who on being shown the front legs, while the back legs were concealed, would ever expect to find the latter united in the same whole with the former?' He goes on, 'The reason why cabinet-makers are in the habit of bestowing so much work on the straight legs of chairs and benches, and so little on those which are curved, is that the straight legs are readily ornamented at a cheap rate in the turning lathe; whereas all the ornament that is bestowed on the curved leg must be carved by hand, at great expense.'

'The great fault is the deviation from simplicity. The cause of this fault is that, in London, so great has been the demand for cabinet furniture, and so ardent the desire for novelty, that the great and incessant efforts of the upholsterers are directed to the production of something new; and that this demand for novelty, instead of being met by taste and invention adequate to the supply, has only called forth mechanical changes or combinations of forms.'

Many of the designs resemble the plates in the works of Brown, the Nicholsons and George Smith and apparently, as will be seen, were drawn also from the work of J. B. Papworth (1775–1847) the architect of country houses and picturesque cottages who also made many designs for silver and metalwork, some in the Egyptian taste, during the middle and late Regency. There is even the well-known writing-desk from the 1808 edition of Smith's book, a design repeated in the *Repository* for 1810. Even the austere influence of Hope was not altogether lost in these latter days of undisciplined styles which Loudon felt it his duty to correct.

Commenting on Elizabethan furniture, then being strongly advocated for villas, he wrote, showing at the same time designs for chairs reproduced from Hope's *Household Furniture*: 'There is no one who would not be desirous of possessing a chair both of the Grecian and the Elizabethan kind; but the Elizabethan chair would be valued merely as a curious piece of antiquity: while the other would be prized for its expression, for its suitableness as a seat, for its simplicity, and for the great effect produced in it by a very few lines. This effect of the Grecian chair being independent of historical associations, since it is, in fact, merely an imaginary composition, results wholly from the beauty of the design. A chair in the Tudor style . . . wants that beauty of simplicity, or that evidence of affecting the most important ends by the simplest means, which the Grecian chair displays, and which indeed is characteristic of the whole of Grecian art.'

Not only the influence of Hope was recalled, but the vitalizing inspiration of Charles Heathcote Tatham. In 1842 Joseph Gwilt (1784–1863) wrote in his *Dictionary of Architecture* that the influence of Percier and Fontaine in France 'was paralleled by that of Tatham. To him, perhaps more than to any other person, may be attributed the rise of the Anglo-Greek style which still prevails, as shown in LOUDON ''Encyclopaedia of Cottage, etc., Architecture''. A very large number of the specimens given in that publication may be taken as copies, more or less close, of articles designed by the late J. B. Papworth to exhibit a simplicity of which it was said in 1822 ''the English is more chaste than the French-Greek, and has advanced so rapidly during the last ten years that the French have adopted much of it''.' It is thus that those great innovators of style in the Regency period, Tatham and Hope, were remembered at the opening of a new and profoundly different era in furniture design.

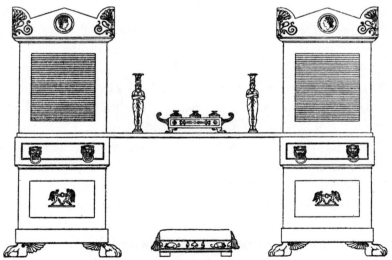

Fig. 8. Design by Thomas Hope for a writing-table. (See Plate 19.)

TYPES OF FURNITURE

CHAIRS

The French origins of the classical Regency chair are found in those made by Georges Jacob for Rambouillet in 1785, and for David's studio in 1788. They derive from 'Etruscan' or late Greek vase-paintings, especially from Herculaneum and Pompeii, and although the French models possess much austere dignity, none of them surpasses in beauty such English examples as the gilt armchairs provided by Holland for Southill, or the most refined and graceful examples of the Trafalgar chair.

The principal characteristics of classical chair design are found in the strongly swept legs, though straight front legs were often combined with curved rear legs; in the use of animal figures, such as the griffon and chimera as leg and arm-supports (Plates 41A, 42A), and in the shape of the backs. These were of two principal types, one, the scroll-back, frequently known in France as the crozier-back (*dossier crossé*) from the scrolled shape of a bishop's crozier (Plates 3, 38B, 39A and title-page). Such chairs, made by Georges Jacob for Fontainebleau in 1792, are to be seen in the Musée de Marmottan. More strongly typical of the Grecian chair is the arc-back (*dossier cintré*) with a broad curved yoke sweeping beyond the side-supports, most frequently combined with swept front and back-legs (Plates 12A, 12B and Fig. 7). A chair of this kind is to be seen in David's painting the *Return of Brutus* of 1789, or in one of the drawings of Lady Hamilton made by Frederick Rehberg in 1794 (Fig. 9). A similar chair to the one illustrated (Plate 12B), closely following a design by Hope, and painted in 'Etruscan' fashion in red and black, is in the Victoria and Albert Museum. The arc-back chair with swept legs is often referred to as a 'curule' chair, but the term should perhaps more properly be applied to one with cross-framed supports (Plate 38A) based on the design of the curule seat, the '*sella curulis*' of the Roman senators. This in fact was not a chair but a cross-framed stool without arms or back, as seen in the designs of Tatham and Hope.

As we have seen, in the early Regency swept rear-legs were combined with turned front-legs of Louis Seize pattern, as in the Southill and Hartwell examples

(Plates 3, 5). Chairs with curved front-legs fall into two distinctive groups. One, the earlier type to evolve, having front-legs of square — or nearly square — section, the front and side-rails being similar, the former tenoned into the legs so as to present a smooth front line and the latter being straight forming a flat side to the seat. The back of such chairs are usually of scroll form, the yoke shaped as a curved strip between the back-supports. As with other chairs, the backs display endless invention in the shaping of yokes, panels and rails (Plate 39A).

The second type of swept-leg chair is one of the most distinctive kinds of furniture evolved during the Regency. In this the curving legs are of oblong-section, much thinner than in the foregoing type, the narrower side to the front, and with the edges rounded. This is the true 'scimitar' or 'sabre'-leg. The front rail is usually set back from the face of the front-leg by a small amount and the side-rails are curved, presenting the characteristic and lovely feature of this style of chair, which is the continuous sweep of line from the curve of the front-legs through curving side-rails up through swept back-supports to the yoke. This is either arc-shaped or in the form of a turned rail shaped to the curve of the sitter's back and worked with a rope or cable moulding in allusion to the victories at sea of the British fleet (Plate 39B). Although the term 'Trafalgar chair' was sometimes given rather loosely to chairs of a differing kind, probably because they came from the 'Trafalgar Workshops' of Morgan & Sanders,[1] this is the type of chair most often known by the name.

The first published design approaching that of the Trafalgar chair is in Sheraton's *Cabinet Encyclopaedia* of 1804–6. This, however, has an arc-back and the knees of the chair have not yet developed the simple rounded line which became typical. The front leg is curved, but the knee is formed with a scroll, probably deriving from the small console scrolls that appear at the tops of the legs of chairs made by Georges Jacob and by the *ébénistes* Bovo and C. Séné *le jeune* in the Louis Quinze and Seize periods. In fact, such scrolls are seen much earlier, in chairs of Louis Quatorze style. The form of the Trafalgar chair was fully developed by 1805, and remained popular until about 1815, and, indeed, much later. They were used almost exclusively as 'parlour-chairs', that is, as chairs for the dining-parlour, and they were frequently made of beech and painted black or bronze-green in allusion to their classical exemplars having been made of bronze. Later in the Regency, Grecian chairs were painted, or stained with vitriol and polished, to represent rosewood. The Trafalgar chair nearly always had a caned seat with a loose squab cushion, fastened underneath by tapes.

[1] See p.57.

Chairs in France were made with swept front legs and rounded knees, but not until after 1815, for it appears that the original development of this type was due to English genius.

An especially graceful variant of the early Regency chair was the type in which the side-rail and back-supports were in one sweeping curve, the forward end turning upwards in a small scroll, and with the front and back legs curving downwards in an opposing semi-circular curve. Chairs of this type were shown in the *Repository* for October 1815, but were in use about ten years earlier.

A distinctive later Regency development was the curved back-yoke having the ends shaped in a spiral volute and with small leaf capitals marking the join with the back-supports. The top edge of the yoke often has also a little scroll. Chairs embodying this feature were made by Gillow for Broughton Hall between 1811 and 1813 at a price of $2\frac{1}{2}$ guineas each.[1] The later development of the classical chair-back, which carried the Trafalgar chair in continued popularity to the middle of Victoria's reign, and is found associated with curved scimitar-legs up to that time, is the type of arc-back having the ends of the yoke curving strongly outwards, sometimes finished at the top corner with a scroll or patera (Plate 41B). The type is illustrated in Smith's last book, but seems first to have appeared in England about 1812, in chairs supplied to the Prince Regent, although the type probably originated with Georges Jacob about 1788.

Chair-backs of extravagant scrolled design, sometimes with prominent shell or honeysuckle cresting, or fore-shadowing the lively curves of neo-Rococo developments, appear in the later issues of the *Repository* and in Henry Whitaker's *Cabinet and Upholstery Furniture* of 1825.

Drawing-room chairs were more elaborate than parlour chairs and were made of mahogany or painted and gilt. The legs, if swept, were usually of square-section, but turned legs were frequently found. The side-rails were straight and the seats usually stuffed. In the late Regency the square legs were made thick and stumpy in proportion and with a much slighter curve than earlier. The same development is found in late Empire furniture. Some handsome drawing-room chairs, carved and painted white, and gilt, were made for the Duke of Northumberland by the firm of Morrel & Hughes in 1825, and were of this character. They were described in the *Repository* for March of that year as 'covered in satin in gold colours on a light blue ground', and are to be seen to-day in the hall at Syon House.*

Chairs with animal monopodia or terminal figures forming the front-legs or the

[1] Hussey in *Country Life*, 14 April 1950.

arm-supports were illustrated by Sheraton in his *Dictionary* and *Encyclopaedia* (Plate 41A), and later were strongly favoured by Thomas Hope and George Smith, following the example of the proto-Empire chairs designed by Georges Jacob about 1788 and by J. B. Séné about 1797. Chairs embodying such motifs were intended chiefly as drawing-room or library chairs (Plates 41A, 42A).

Spoon-back or gondola chairs were popular all through the Regency. They first appear in David's painting the *Return of Brutus*. A design in the *Repository* for December 1809, shows one of this type with curved square-section legs, and ornaments of honeysuckle and bolt-heads in gilt metal, also as seen in David's paintings.

The curricle chair was so called by Sheraton in the *Cabinet Dictionary* of 1803, after the tub-shaped carriage of that time. It remained popular throughout the Regency as a library or reading chair.

A type of chair which intrigues collectors is the reading- or conversation-chair, the back of which had a narrow support to enable the user to sit astride and lean his arms upon the back. The top rail was made flat for this purpose and sometimes had a book-rest for reading, and folding brackets for candles. The arms of chairs also display interesting phases in their evolution during the Regency period. In the last years of the eighteenth century, under the surviving influence of Hepplewhite and early Sheraton designs, the arms were set high on the backs of the chairs, and were of slender proportions. They swept downwards to the seat either in one piece at a sharp angle, or joining an upright arm-support, sometimes by means of a bobbin-like feature, or a small scroll, or even the head of a ram or lion (Plate 41B).

One of the most distinctive Regency developments which was general by 1805, is the chair-arm in the form of a bold scroll curving downwards and inwards with the bottom of the scroll resting on the side-rail (Plate 40). This robust form seems to be entirely English and does not appear in French Empire furniture until after it is seen in English examples. The first recorded instance of it is apparently in the mahogany and gilt settee made about 1794 for Carlton House. A more elegant shape of arm in the early Regency, however, is one of Etruscan type in which the arm sweeps forward and downwards to meet an inward curving support, as in the gilt armchairs at Southill (Plates 3, 38B). The earliest appearance of this form seems to be in the mahogany hall-seats made for the Brighton Pavilion by Elward, Marsh and Tatham in 1801 (Plate 2B). An intermediate form is the short arm which joins an inward-curving support by means of a bobbin-like knob (Plate 41A).

They are found in drawing-room chairs made by Gillow in 1803 for Broughton Hall.[1]

Backs of chairs gave opportunities for endless variations of design, in panels and interlaced lattice forms, but in general the distinctive trend was away from the vertical emphasis of the late eighteenth-century chairs (Plate 38B) to a horizontal tendency (Plates 39A, 39B).

In the last decade of the eighteenth century chairs had often been made with slender, tapering turned legs, with the ends slightly swept forward, but this was gradually displaced by the curved leg, though the former by no means disappeared. From the publication of George Smith's book in 1808 turned legs became increasingly common, especially for drawing-room chairs, and ultimately almost supplanted the oblong or square-section swept leg. By July 1813, the *Repository* is showing in a ladies' fashion-plate a chair with very thick turned legs, and ten years later they are universal, and often shown with long lambrequins or drooping leaf-shaped ornaments on the legs.

In 1822 Richard Brown wrote of chairs, 'This article has lately undergone a far greater improvement than any other branch of the cabinet art, inasmuch as it now baffles the most skilful artist to produce any new forms.' In the late Regency the sabre-leg, of thin oblong-section, almost vanished, and Grecian parlour-chairs were once more commonly made with tapering turned and curved legs. The cheaper types were of beech, painted or stained and polished in imitation of rosewood. In 1833 they sold in London for 7s. to 12s. each.[2]

PAINTED CHAIRS

Painted chairs form an important category of Regency furniture. They are described in the *Repository* for August 1814, as 'intended for best bed chambers, for secondary drawing rooms, and occasionally to serve for routs'.

Foremost are the better quality chairs intended for the dining-parlour, especially of the Trafalgar type, made of beech and painted black or bronze-green, or to represent rosewood or mahogany. Also of good quality are those made by Elward, Marsh and Tatham of beech, painted to simulate bamboo. They incorporate subtleties of design such as carefully shaped back-legs and a 'wrap-round' treatment for the caned seat deriving from the Chinese split-bamboo technique. An

---

[1] Hussey, op. cit.
[2] Loudon, *Encyclopaedia of Cottage, Farm and Villa Architecture and Furniture*, 1833.

especially charming feature is a device in the under-framing or in the back of these chairs consisting of two members curving towards each other and separated by balls (Plate 44). Another grade of painted chairs, probably made in Buckingham-shire, is distinguished by having seats in the form of broad, flat frames with turned legs set well underneath. These were often used in less important rooms, especially bedrooms. Many chairs of both these grades were used at the Royal Pavilion,* and in bedrooms at Uppark, Sussex.*

Some painted chairs had rush-seats. They are shown in a ladies' fashion-plate in the *Repository* for 1815. Certain spindly, mechanical and spiritless types of imitation bamboo chairs of a light kind, especially the sort of gilded chairs that are frequently seen in dress salons and provided for seating by caterers at fashion-able functions, are of a kind belonging to the period 1850 to 1870 and have been reproduced more or less continuously since.

WINDSOR CHAIRS

The Windsor chair-making industry, centred in Buckinghamshire and active since the seventeenth century, was flourishing in Regency times and produced great quantities of chairs for kitchens, bedrooms, dining-rooms and gardens. No conclusive reason for the adoption of the name 'Windsor' has been discovered.

High Wycombe was one of the important centres of the industry at this time, chair-making having been started at Marlow Hill in 1805 by Samuel Treacher, as a winter occupation for his farm-hands. At High Wycombe Thomas Widginton organized the assembly of chairs by this semi-skilled labour with parts supplied by the local fresh craftsmen or 'bodgers' who made the turned legs on primitive pole-lathes, and in 1810 he set up the first furniture manufactory in the town.[1]

Many of the Windsor chairs had a simple elegance, and embodied some of the characteristic decorative motifs of the day, including a fretted form of the Prince of Wales's feathers at the end of the eighteenth century and the beginning of the nineteenth. A distinctive feature of the Windsor chair was the 'tablet' seat, shaped from a single piece of elm with the adze and carefully hollowed for comfort. Arms made in a single piece with the back-rail and curving forward to join a forward-curving arm support at a sharp angle, formed another marked characteristic (Plate 43B). These are features which have survived in Windsor chairs to this day.

[1] Roe, *Windsor Chairs*, 1953.

STOOLS, WINDOW SEATS AND FOOTSTOOLS

Stools or tabourets are among the most beautiful objects of the Regency period, because some of the loveliest forms were chosen for their design, and there was often a combination in them of the most successful decorative motifs, for their principal purpose was to serve 'as ornamental and extra Seats in elegant Drawing Rooms'.[1]

Although box-shaped stools were used at Southill, the cross-framed design was almost universal and gave endless opportunities for graceful invention in the designing of the supports. One especially elegant form has slender round supports and arms shaped as opposing semi-circles, the crossing marked by a lotus or palm-leaf ornament. The ends of the arm-rests were shaped as lion- or swans'-heads, and the feet as lion-paws or similar forms (Plate 15A).

George Smith's early designs for stools follow those of Thomas Hope very closely, especially those based on animal forms such as the griffon, and Hope's design with crossed swords was also imitated. Stools making use of Egyptian motifs are among the most successful and charming examples of the furniture of this style (Plate 16A).

The coverings of stools were often rich and luxurious, being frequently of velvet or satin and fitted with a fringe and tassels.

Window seats were longer than ordinary stools and showed to especial advantage when set before the long windows reaching down to floor level that were popular in the Regency (Plate 43A).

Footstools are much smaller and were often square, with feet in the form of classical ornaments such as the honeysuckle (Plate 3). A scrolled shape was also popular, usually derived from classical console designs like those of Tatham. By 1813 small lion-shaped feet were appearing in footstools. The usual coverings were leather, velvet, or printed cloth 'suitable to the apartment'[2] (Plate 42B).

Stools with dolphin-shaped bases, and seats in the form of a shell, richly and entirely gilded, are occasionally to be found and were intended chiefly for decorative effect in halls and reception rooms.

[1] G. Smith, *A Collection of Designs for Household Furniture and Interior Decoration*, 1808.
[2] G. Smith, op. cit.

SETTEES, SOFAS AND COUCHES

The settee has been regarded as distinct from the sofa in being an extension of the armchair, with slender legs of the chair type, whereas the sofa has evolved from the day-bed and is made with a long frame mounted on more heavily proportioned supports. However, the familiar distinction is a loose one and Sheraton consistently called a piece of the former type a sofa.

Early in the new century the growing passion for reviving not merely the decorative themes of classical antiquity but also its social manners and customs, elevated the Grecian couch from which ancient philosophers had discoursed to an important place in the furnishing of rooms. With the image of Madame Recamier, as depicted in 1800 by the French painter David, in her mind, the newly liberated woman of the Regency adopted the sofa as the throne from which to rule her intellectual and domestic realm.

The sofa was judged no less necessary for gentlemen. According to the *Repository* for July 1809, 'Amongst the various decorations of a library, a sofa is an indispensable article of furniture; it not only ornaments, but becomes a comfort when tired and fatigued with study, writing and reading — the exhausted mind can only be recruited by rest . . . in no other country in the world is such complete convenience and comfort to be found as in England.'

The first published designs for the fully developed Grecian sofa appear in Sheraton's *Cabinet Dictionary* of 1803 in both popular forms; the kind with one high end, a small scroll at the foot and a short scrolled arm-rest; and that with ends of equal height and a continuous straight back (Plates 46A, 46B). Both types persisted well into Victorian times, with variations of detail and with fluctuating felicity of design. Sofas were found to lend themselves conveniently to the display of animal forms and George Smith's earlier work as well as Sheraton's later volumes give many more or less extravagant examples. Some sofas were made with high straight ends faced with pilasters, decorated with classical ornament. This type appeared early at Southill (Plate 5) and continued to be popular in the 1820's, when designs for them appeared in the *Repository*, and George Smith illustrates the theme in 1828.

From 1812 onwards it became common for the back-rail of a double-ended sofa to have a central ornament or cresting boldly carved with a pattern of honeysuckle or leaves, or a shell motif (Plates 32A, 46B, 47B) as in the days of Louis Quatorze

99

and William Kent. This characteristically late feature is seen as early as 1810 in sofas and chairs made for Carlton House by Tatham and Bailey. Another late tendency was for the graceful outward-sweeping classical legs to be replaced by straight legs of various forms, finely carved lion legs being found in some examples, and turned straight legs, often with gadroon ornament, on other instances (Plates 32A, 46A). After the Restoration, when the full-blown designs of the French Empire were increasingly fashionable, the form of the classical sofa in England tended generally to become debased by enlargement of the proportions and by ponderous ornament (Plate 92B).

Chaises-longues began early in the century as arm-chairs with an integral forward extension. Later the term *chaise-longue* passed more and more out of use, the word couch being more frequently used to describe a small sofa with one high end and a plain foot.

COMMODES AND DWARF CABINETS

In the opening days of the Regency the commode was a delicately proportioned article deriving from the elegant and influential form of the French *commodes ouvertes* of the Louis Seize *ébénistes*, the type of which was already represented in this country by the Carlton House pier-tables (Plate 2A). The designs of Sheraton in the *Dictionary* and *Encyclopaedia* are based on models of this kind.

In fact the light commodes, dwarf cupboards, open cabinets and bookcases of this type form one of the largest of all classes of early Regency furniture, embodying enchanting varieties of detail. An extremely handsome French commode by Weisweiler of about 1780 (Plate 48) reveals the Louis Seize ancestry of such familiar features of Regency furniture as the tapering fluted columns with hollowed capitals and peg-top feet as well as embodying the basic form of innumerable light cabinets, commodes and dwarf bookcases of English design (Plates 49, 50A, 51).

Commodes of a more imposing sort were far less common, both in this country and in France, until after the first decade of the century. There are few designs for such pieces in Percier and Fontaine, and none at all in Thomas Hope's book. The furniture of antiquity had no precedents for the massive commode.

A distinctive characteristic of the period was the preference for grille-fronted doors backed with pleated silk instead of solid panels, and this feature is among the most beautiful aspects of Regency furniture, especially when the grilles are of curvilinear and interlaced design. They derive from the wire fronts of eighteenth-century cupboard and bookcase doors, which were usually of common wire, although about the end of the century these were being made in varied and delightful interlacing patterns. At the same time grilles began to be made of thick square-section brass, crossing diagonally in lattice form, with small brass bosses at the junction (Plate 50A). This pattern was a favourite one throughout the Regency (Plate 53). From 1800 onwards curvilinear patterns came into use.

Another delightful pattern of grille was in the form of a wire border, with classical ornament, especially honeysuckle motifs, at the angles and with rosettes also appearing (Plate 50B). This form is of French origin, and became more elaborate in late Regency examples, the open panels being filled with scrolling acanthus designs and such motifs as lyres.

The typical Empire formula of a shallow cupboard flanked by marble or mahogany columns with gilt capitals was a late development, appearing in English furniture about 1812 and after. The gilt metal ornament of the doors of the piece illustrated is an early instance of a kind of decoration more fully developed in one of Smith's designs for commodes[1] (Plate 50B).

A few large commodes had been made in France from the beginning of the century by *ébénistes* like the Jacob Frères and Alexandre Maigret, with sparse classical metal decoration on mahogany or with the gilt sphinx-headed pilasters of the Egyptian enthusiasm, but articles of this form were not common in France till after the Restoration, when large commodes in late Empire style made by the *ébénistes* Desmalter, Werner and Bénard became numerous, and similar articles became popular in this country also, and indeed are among the distinctive forms of late Regency taste. Designs for handsome commodes and buffets inspired from French sources appeared in the *Repository* in the later Regency years, and are also prominent in Smith's final volume and other late design books. Many of such pieces displayed the motifs and decoration of the revived Louis Quatorze style, and in others the quality of cabinet-work was subordinate to the richness of panels painted with naturalistic flower subjects in the manner introduced by Jacob-Desmalter in France about 1824[2] (Plate 37). These paintings, which were on paper applied to the cabinet fronts, have much in common with the large flower-paintings on great ceremonial vases of Sèvres porcelain made in the late Empire or at the Restoration.[3]

[1] G. Smith, *The Cabinet-Maker's and Upholsterer's Guide*, 1828.
[2] Illustrated in Nicolay, *Maîtres ébénistes français*, 1956, p. 483, Fig. F.   [3] See also p. 136.

Difficulties of nomenclature for all these types of furniture were just as puzzling in the Regency as they are to-day. Robert Southey asked in 1816[1], 'commodes, console tables . . . chiffoniers, what are all these?' and could find no person in the house to answer him.

DWARF BOOKCASES

Dwarf bookcases were chiefly used in drawing-rooms or other living-rooms. They differ little in form from commodes and dwarf cabinets, except in having open shelves, or doors with open grilles, instead of solid or silk-panelled doors, although Smith describes both types indiscriminately as commodes and dwarf bookcases (Plate 36). A circular form for small, low bookcases was especially favoured (Plate 77A). The round table top was sometimes fitted with drawers, and occasionally with a brass gallery.

CHIFFONIERS

Closely allied to the commode in the scheme of Regency furniture is the chiffonier, its form deriving again from the archetypal Louis Seize *commodes ouvertes*, but having open shelves instead of cupboards, and a superstructure of shelves (Plate 6).

The chiffonier passed through an inglorious phase in its debased Victorian form, but the design has been revived in our own day for the functional virtues of the curved open shelves of bookcases, room-dividers and kitchen-fitments.

The term *chiffonier* is of mid-eighteenth century French derivation. Havard describes it as a piece containing many drawers for the storage of books, papers, jewels and 'chiffons',[2] but before the end of the century it had assumed the characteristic open form, with a superstructure of shelves, and was intended for the display of porcelain and other small objects.

With one or more shelves added, the commode with a closed front becomes the commode-chiffonier, so called by George Smith. Later examples of the commode-chiffonier gave opportunities for the use of the popular Regency device of shelf-supports in the form of a scroll, sometimes of a rounded shape, but more

---

[1] Southey, *Letters from England*, 1957.   [2] Havard, *Dictionnaire de l'ameublement*, 1887, p. 806.

frequently of robust square-section. This feature, found in many Regency pieces, is one that may have developed through the ease with which its production was adapted to large-scale factory production (Plate 53).

PIER-TABLES, CONSOLE-TABLES AND SIDE-TABLES

As their name implies, pier-tables were intended to stand before the piers or narrow sections of walls between windows. The type had been in use since early in the eighteenth century. Their tops were shallow, so as not to project into the room, and were often made of marble (Plate 52A) or scagliola or, in the more modest examples, painted in imitation of marble. The pre-Regency examples had delicate legs and fanciful stretchers below in the manner of Robert Adam and Louis Seize specimens and Sheraton continued to illustrate this type as late as 1801. As we have seen, the pier-tables that Sheraton saw in 1793 at Carlton House were almost certainly French but their form was closely followed years afterwards, as it was for similar types of furniture.

In the earlier examples the legs were turned and gilded, with rather prominent ornaments in the fashion of French colonnettes, but from 1805 onwards the characteristic Regency type of column, divided in the middle and decorated with elegant motifs of lotus leaves and water-leaves were more frequently seen (Plate 52B). Later still the supports were shaped as formal classical columns, most frequently Corinthian in the late Regency.

From the publication of Thomas Hope's work in 1807 and George Smith's *Household Furniture* of 1808 onwards, the type of pier-table with animal monopodia supports became popular, frequently with only a single support. A design in the latter volume embodies an elaborate form of the typical late Regency scroll-shaped supports for the bases, as well as for the upper shelves.

In the later Regency, as indicated in Smith's volume of 1829, pier-tables had become more ponderous and, though the basic form differed little from the earlier types, there were usually only two supports, and were of sturdier proportions.

The definition of console-, pier- and side-tables was as puzzling to Robert Southey as for commodes and chiffoniers (see page 102). Side-tables are used against the wall of a room, and stand independently upon their legs. Console-tables are those which are dependent for some of their support upon the wall, either actually or ostensibly, and have their main support in front only. Any support at the back is given by plain unobtrusive uprights. Side-tables or console-tables for halls and reception rooms only differ from dining-room sideboard-tables in having no back-rail, and having tops of marble instead of polished wood. An especially splendid example in the Victoria and Albert Museum* has a top formed of various specimen marbles, and finely shaped console supports with foliate ornament. Articles of this kind in the revived Louis Quatorze manner were greatly in favour during the late Regency, and appear in George Smith's last work (Plate 33A).

SOFA-TABLES AND GAMES-TABLES

The sofa-table has long been regarded as being among the most attractive types of Regency furniture. It seems to have been a wholly British invention, owing nothing to French influence. Its beauty of form and convenience for modern use, whether for its original purpose or as a dressing- or writing-table, or even as an intimate dining table, causes it to be sought after more than almost any other type. Throughout the Regency it provided endless opportunities for delightful invention in the design of the supports, for excellence of craftsmanship and variety of decorative treatment.

The name derives obviously from the fact that it was intended to stand before, or even behind, a sofa, and thus to serve as the hub and centre of the domestic life of upper and middle-class women during the Regency.

In the early Sheraton period sofa-tables were made with flat end-supports, often vase-shaped in outline and on curved, splayed feet. After 1800 the vase-shaped supports gave place to plain, flat, straight-sided members (Plate 58), and a little later lyre-shaped ends, consisting of a pair of curved members, came into vogue (Plate 61). In the early Regency simple turned supports were often used. Stretchers varied in design, a rectangular section often being used with plain flat ends (Plate 58). In some examples the stretcher is formed as a high arch or a pair of curved tie-pieces or brackets take its place, joining the end supports to the underside of the table. Turned stretchers were commonly used with many types of support (Plate 61). The raised and rounded knees to legs which are found in the later types of small tables first appeared quite early in Sheraton's *Cabinet Encyclopaedia* but the kind with a hooked upper curve were seen about 1815 (Plates 59, 61, 63). Cross-shaped end-supports were occasionally used for sofa-tables, but were more often adopted for writing tables, which needed a firm, broad-based support (Plates 9B, 76B). Lion monopodia supports were characteristic devices of George Smith in his 1808 volume (Plates 22A, 22B)

About 1812 sofa-tables on a single central support began to supplant the earlier type and again much variety is seen in their design. An elegant early form consisted of four slender columns on a centre platform and splayed feet (Plate 59). Another, probably deriving from the classical pedestal tables of Thomas Hope, had a central pedestal with concave sides (Plate 63). A little later the turned pillar on a claw base, with a circular, square or concave-sided platform appeared (Plate 62). From about 1815 deep U-shaped supports were in use.

From about 1820 onwards, vase-shaped end-supports again came into favour, but now with concave sides and thin-waisted, sometimes in a solid piece, but often made with a pair of thin curving members, the waist joined by a boss. Also at this time straight end-supports on flat bases, with lion-paw feet, as seen in Hope's work, were again fashionable and the best examples of the period exhibit the finely drawn and carved foliate ornament typical of the time.

The sofa-table was often adapted to serve as a combined writing-table by means of a reversible sliding centre-portion covered with leather on one side. A combined sofa-games-table was made with the reversible portion inlaid with squares of light and dark wood to form a chess or draughts-board. In these combined tables a well beneath the slide, inlaid with the markings of a backgammon board and provided with receptacles for counters, replaced the drawers.

Distinctive, and indeed in the early Regency, essential features of sofa-tables were the flaps, which were placed at the ends, instead of at the sides as with Pembroke tables. In the late Regency the end-flaps disappeared, and the term sofa-table was used only as an alternative name for the 'occasional table' with the top in a single piece (Plate 64). In his last volume Smith uses the term only in this latter sense, and had no design for the sofa-table with flaps.

PEMBROKE TABLES

Jane Austen, writing about 1804 in her unfinished story *The Watsons* of a 'circle of smart people . . . arranged with all the honours of visiting round the fire', described 'Miss Watson seated at the best Pembroke Table with the best tea-things before her'. All through Regency days the Pembroke table, with four legs and flaps at the sides supported by hinged wooden brackets, retained its popularity, but the top was almost invariably of rectangular shape with rounded corners instead of displaying the variety of oval or oblong forms with serpentine edges given to it in the Hepplewhite and early Sheraton periods. They were frequently made of solid mahogany and in the early Regency the legs were usually turned, with simple ringed, bamboo-like ornaments. After 1820 the turning of the legs became more elaborate and tasteless.

This type of Pembroke table continued in popularity well into Victorian times, but an important development was the adoption about 1812 of the central pedestal base instead of the customary four legs, when it resembled some forms of sofa-table except that the flaps were at the sides and the drawers at the ends, instead of the reverse (Plate 78B).

CARD-TABLES

Card-tables were made with the tops to fold in half, usually with the playing surface covered with baize or leather. They were intended to stand against the walls of a room when not in use for card-play, and then served as occasional tables. With polished tops they are sometimes known and used as tea-tables.

When in September 1801, Fanny Burney was furnishing Camilla Cottage and asked her father for a small present, she chose 'a sort of table for a little work and a few books, *en gala* — without which a room always looks forlorn'. Dr. Burney gave her a pair of card-tables which, it was agreed, would 'do a thousand times better than any *Tavolina*'.

During the Regency the Hepplewhite and Sheraton type of card-table on four slender, tapering square legs gave place to tables on central supports with splayed legs that were sometimes, but not invariably, made to open outwards on hinges to provide support for the large table top. Such tables display a variety of designs for the central supports surpassing in their profusion those of sofa-tables (Plate 65).

OCCASIONAL AND QUARTETTO TABLES

The casual arrangement of furniture which displaced the formal lay-out of eighteenth-century interiors was in vogue before the end of the century, and Lord Torrington wrote disapprovingly in his *Diary*[1] of 'little skuttling tables being

[1] *Torrington Diary*, 1792.

brought before a hearth'. A few years later, in 1801, Fanny Burney considered that 'no room looks really comfortable, or even quite furnished, without two tables — one to keep the wall and take upon itself the dignity of a little tidyness, the other to stand here, there and everywhere, and hold letters, and make the agreeable'[1] [*sic*].

The occasional tables which filled these needs were made in a wide range of forms and decorative styles. Some were on tripod stands, others on four columns (Plate 88A) or with animal-headed supports. Many examples had end-supports of lyre and other designs. They were also made in the form of miniature drum-top tables or *étagères*.

Quartetto tables, illustrated in Sheraton's *Cabinet Dictionary* (Plate 9A), continued for many years to be made in the form of four small tables nesting together, and with variations of detail according to fashion and period, the early ones with four slender legs turned in 'bamboo' fashion; with lyre-shaped supports in the mid-Regency, and later with the concave-sided, narrow-waisted supports of that time.

TEA-POYS AND WORK-TABLES

Tea-poys were described by Smith in 1808 as 'used in Drawing-rooms, &c. to prevent the company rising from their seats when taking refreshment'. The term tea-poy is properly applied to a small pedestal tea-table, but later in the Regency it came to be used for tea-caddies on stands, usually in the form of a square box with a lid, mounted on a pedestal, and holding containers for various kinds of tea and a bowl for sugar (Plate 34B). They were favourite objects for decoration with brass-inlay from about 1812 onwards, and the later examples were often japanned or made in Tunbridge Ware inlay.

Work-tables were made in the form of a small table on a pair of supports, similar to a sofa-table, but having a silk bag or pouch, usually pleated, hanging in a space below a sliding or lifting top. They were also frequently made in a similar manner to the later Regency tea-poy, or caddy on a stand, in the shape of a box on a pedestal (Plate 34A) or pair of lyre-shaped supports, and like them were often the subject of brass-inlay decoration. Japanned work-tables were made in various

[1] F. Burney, letter of 6 September 1801, quoted in Constance Hill's *Juniper Hall*, p. 258.

forms, but were sold in novelty shops like the 'Temple of Fancy',[1] rather than at cabinet-makers' establishments.

PEDESTALS, LAMP AND VASE STANDS

Pedestals played an essential part in the life of the Regency period, being necessary for carrying lamps and candelabra, as well as being used for supporting busts, vases and flower-baskets. The solid square-section, tapering type of classical pedestal was little used during the Regency, having been common in the days of William Kent, Chippendale and Robert Adam in the eighteenth century. Sheraton illustrated only the delicate tripod-stand for lights of the Adam period.

The precedents adopted by Thomas Hope a few years later, including designs published by Tatham, encouraged such forms as the classical tripod and the columnar pedestal (Plate 20B) both on triangular bases, and stands with animal supports such as lion-monopodia (Plate 20A). There were stands for small lamps shaped as slender straight shafts on a base of three animal feet.

The designs for pedestals provided by Smith in his earlier work were said to be 'appropriate for Busts and Statues, they are equally useful in halls and on staircases, and need not be rejected in drawing-rooms, if executed in wood carved and gilt, in which case they answer conveniently to support vases of flowers, or figures carrying branches for lights'. They were intended to be made in wood painted in imitation of marble. Smith also recommended pedestals, or 'candelabri' as he called them, to stand in the corners of drawing-rooms either for candelabra or to carry alabaster or glass vases containing lights.[2] Plain cylindrical column pedestals were often made of scagliola, and in middle-class households wooden tripod-stands for lamps and candelabra were popular in a great variety of forms with column supports and splayed standards (Plate 89B).

FIRE-SCREENS

The general form of fire-screens remained unchanged for over a hundred years from the late eighteenth century. The cheval-screen, on a pair of supports, was intended to stand on the hearth before the fireplace, and the pole-screen or

---

[1] See p. 136.   [2] G. Smith, 1808.

tripod-screen for the purpose of shielding the face of someone sitting near the fire.

The early Hepplewhite and Sheraton cheval-screens were of great delicacy, made of satinwood, and carrying oval, shield-shaped or lyre-shaped panels between a pair of uprights. Later, more rectilinear forms were used, and in 1808 George Smith described drawing-room cheval-screens with 'frames to slide out on the sides, covered with plain coloured stuff'. During the middle Regency cheval-screens were usually of fairly simple design, the oblong frame being of narrow section, the front edge worked with a hollow filled with a gold line, and the sliding panel made to draw upwards. The supports were made in the current style of the period, with plain splayed feet in the earlier years, and later on with more elaborately shaped feet, possibly with foliated carving.

The main form of the pole-screen also remained unchanged for many years, the only modification being in the character of details as fashions changed. In the early Regency the Hepplewhite and Sheraton designs survived, of oval, heart-shaped or shield-shaped panels upon a slender pole, supported on delicate tripod feet. The panels were made to contain embroidery or painted decorations behind glass, or they were formed of wooden panels without frames, oblong, octagonal or otherwise simply shaped, painted with classical Wedgwood-like designs.

Under the influence of Thomas Hope a more severe classical influence became apparent. The pole was shaped as a lance, and the screen panel as a Grecian shield, oblong with the corners angled, and painted with some such classical device as 'Jove's fulmen (thunderbolt) as wrought by the Cyclops'. The base of these screens was made as a plain solid circular block. George Smith's shield-shaped screens on pole-stands are like Hope's, but with heavy triangular pedestal bases.

For less rigidly classical interiors tripod-based screens continued in use, showing a great variety of forms in the shaping of the feet, often with animal motifs. From 1815 onwards the banner-screen came into use, having instead of a frame or panel a piece of fabric, perhaps fringed and with a pointed lower edge, hanging like a banner from a transverse rod. Occasionally trumpet-banners bearing the emblems of regiments that had fought at Salamanca, Talavera or Waterloo were used as screen banners, or the richly emblazoned drum cloths or tabards used at the coronation of King George IV were adapted to serve the same purpose.

The carved and gilt cheval-screen on the French model of the early and mid-eighteenth century, of square proportions, with rococo decoration was revived in a florid form in the 1820's, for use in great establishments like Belvoir, Londonderry House and Windsor Castle.

THE WHAT-NOT, MUSIC-STANDS
AND MUSIC-CANTERBURIES

The what-not in its debased late nineteenth-century form, ornamented with ugly turnings and carvings, has long been one of the chief derisory symbols of the cluttered-up Victorian interior. In the early years of its use from about 1800 onwards, it was an article of simple elegance and usefulness.

The what-not is a stand almost square in plan, with four slender corner-posts supporting three, four or more shelves for the display of small objects such as ornaments and curiosities, or for holding books and papers or music (Plate 79B). Frequently the base was made with one or two shallow drawers, or even with a cellaret. The shelves were fitted with a wooden rim in the more modest examples, and with brass galleries in the richer ones. The taller ones were often made with the top shelf to lift up for use as a writing-slope or music-stand. The earlier articles displayed much elegance in the restrained turning of the corner posts, and refined ornament in the form of lotus leaves marking the sections, was often as felicitously used.

Music-stands, often double-sided, and made with candle-holders, offered good opportunities for the use of the favourite Regency theme of a pedestal supported on a tripod base, or in the later instances on a triangular plinth. The fashionable lyre-shape was an obvious choice for the desk portion of music-stands. While the finer specimens were made of mahogany, music-stands were popular objects for decorative treatment by painting, in classical and floral designs, and for japanning with *chinoiserie* motifs, in scarlet and ivory as well as black.

Music-canterburies were spoken of by Sheraton in the *Cabinet Dictionary* as named after the capital of Kent, and as 'a small music-stand, with two or three hollow-topped partitions, framed in slips of mahogany' for holding music books. They were fitted with small legs and castors and 'adapted to run in under a pianoforte'. Later examples were made with curved splayed feet on foliated brass castors (Plate 66B).

THE PIANOFORTE

'The approbation of pianofortes, as instruments of refined entertainment, and the elegance with which they are finished, in the different factories of the Metropolis, have long rendered them an indispensable article for apartments;'. So observed the *Repository* for February 1812, but the characteristic form of the grand pianoforte as we know it to-day was already established long before the Regency, in the shape of the harpsichords of the sixteenth century. Large grand pianofortes were being made by the firm of Broadwood of Great Pulteney Street, Golden Square, London, in mahogany with gilt brass mounts and turned legs before 1820, and the Victoria and Albert Museum possesses an instrument of this kind and date by William Stodart of Golden Square, 'maker to Their Majesties and the Princesses'.

The 'square pianoforte' of the Regency has been immortalized by Thackeray in *Vanity Fair*. The familiar shape derives from much earlier precursors in the virginals and clavichord of the sixteenth century, but the pianoforte action was introduced into England in the 1760's by Johannes Zumpe. Late eighteenth-century square pianos were usually of solid mahogany and were supported on simple frames of four square legs with a plain stretcher. In such instruments as those made by James Ball about 1789 to 1802 square legs were still used, and connected by a shelf-like stretcher with a cut-out front edge. During the Regency the cases were more frequently veneered, sometimes with lines of inlay and cross-banding, and supported on six turned legs screwed directly into the body. After about 1812 the legs became more deeply turned and sometimes heavily ribbed. Often the instruments were decorated with a gilt metal beading round the bottom edge of the case, and with gilt metal capitals to the legs, of rich foliated design in the finer examples, and in the form of an embossed metal band in less splendid instruments. The latter were usually made of plain solid mahogany (Plate 81).

Perhaps the most notable development in the realm of the piano during the Regency was the invention of the upright instrument or 'chamber pianoforte', the result of patents taken out in the late eighteenth century.[1] It was taller and narrower than the modern equivalent, and usually with a pleated silk front to the upper portion. The type was not always represented by graceful and elegant design, and eventually it became more associated with the overpowering heaviness of the Victorian interior.

[1] R.E.M. Harding, *History of the Pianoforte*, 1933.

LIBRARY BOOKCASES

Although small bookcases and sets of shelves were more popular during the Regency than at any other previous time, the great library-bookcase remained, as in the time of Chippendale and Hepplewhite, among the monuments of English taste and style. The library of a house was properly one of the chief shrines of the classical tradition, where the works of Adam, Stuart and Revett, Robert Wood and Thomas Hope were venerated, and many library-bookcases of noble proportions reflected this austere mood of the early years of the century (Plate 68).

The Egyptian taste and the Gothic style were also found to be congenial to the atmosphere of a library and were successfully expressed in many handsome examples. The bookcase of later design with the characteristic boldly carved scrolling and honeysuckle ornament finely represents the absorption of classical detail into the English domestic furniture tradition (Plate 69).

Tall, single-tier bookcases as seen at Althorp* and Southill often derived their form from precursors such as cabinets by the Louis Seize *ébénistes*, J. P. Dusautoy and G. Dester as well as by Jacob and Weisweiler.

LIBRARY-TABLES, WRITING-DESKS AND SECRETAIRES

The monumental library- and writing-table of the years from Chippendale and Robert Adam to the mid-nineteenth century has been one of the characteristic symbols of British culture, and over that time its basic form of two or four large pedestal cupboards with knee-openings between remained virtually unchanged.

In the following years these tables displayed the various typical motifs of current fashionable taste, the austere classical style, and to a lesser extent the Egyptian taste (Plate 71) and the Gothic being especially favoured in the library. A magnificent example of the first kind at the Victoria and Albert Museum has supports in the form of classical female terminal figures, and carved emblems of the *caduceus*, the winged staff of Mercury, upon the cupboard doors. In instances of the Egyptian inclination the place of these features is sometimes taken by sphinx-headed figures and the royal Egyptian *uraeus*. The great library-table at Stourhead* combines the two styles with figures, beautifully carved, both of Greek philosophers and

Egyptians.[1] At Stonor Park, Oxon.,* amongst many other fine examples of Regency furniture is a great library-table having fluted columns with leaf-capitals, and slender brass colonnette supports.

Circular, or drum-top library-tables, with drawers or alternatively spaces for books in the frieze, are interesting for the innumerable variations in the design of their supports, showing a similar development to those of circular breakfast, Loo and drawing-room tables[2] (Plates 72, 73). Rent-tables were also of this type and had the fronts of the drawers inlaid with letters to assist in the arrangement of business papers.

Writing-desks differ from library-tables in being fitted with pedestals of drawers instead of with cupboards. The simple and lovely spirit of Sheraton's style, as seen in the type of desk with oval ends, was combined with the new influences, such as the lion-paw feet now used (Plate 7) in the manner of his *Dictionary* of 1803.

Some writing-desks display the same tendencies of form as in the mid-Regency sideboard in having the side pedestals higher than the centre-portion. This characteristic is carried to an extreme in an important piece deriving from a well-known design of Thomas Hope (Fig. 8). The pedestals have battered (i.e. sloping) sides and coved cornice-mouldings in the manner of pylons at Egyptian or Greek doorways and the tops are fitted with Greek acroters (i.e. statue-platforms) at the angles (Plate 19 & Fig. 8).

The Carlton House variety of writing-table is another of the famous types of Regency elegance and usefulness. First illustrated by Sheraton in 1793, examples were made by Gillow in 1796 and 1798 and, reaching the height of perfection from about 1805 to 1810, the type was still being made, with detail characteristic of the age, in the late 1820's. Consisting of a D-shaped table with one or more levels of shallow drawers on three sides, the most beautiful examples are probably those with slender, tapering turned legs ornamented with tassel-tops and with rings of 'bamboo' turning (Plate 74) or with tapering fluted legs. Later examples have heavier ribbed legs and a more ponderous arrangement of drawers. Ackermann speaks of the title as given to such tables 'from having been first made for the august personage whose correct taste has so classically embellished that beautiful palace'.

There is a distinctive class of Regency writing-table, ranging in size from very large to small, having drawers in the frieze only, and carried on end-supports which express the varying trends of design throughout the period in much the

---

[1] Illustrated by Hussey in *Country Life*, 23 January 1958. [2] See p. 115.

same manner as do the supports of sofa-tables (Plate 70). Writing-tables with curved cross-shaped end-supports (Plate 76B) such as are illustrated in Sheraton's *Cabinet Dictionary*, were also greatly favoured and some of these rival even the best of the sofa-tables as instances of the highest pitch of beauty attained in Regency furniture. Tatham's classical design of table end-supports shaped as pairs of consoles, which Hope and Smith adopted, was used for the fine writing-table in the library at Somerley, Hampshire.[1]

Similar to the early type of dressing-table with a fold-over top is the writing-desk of about 1810 on turned legs, with drawers below, having a concave front to make room for the knees. When the top is opened to reveal the writing-slope a sliding section containing small drawers rises up.

Writing-desks for ladies were still made in the delightful eighteenth-century form of the *bonheur-de-jour*, of small size and standing on slender, elegant legs, with the top opening forward to provide a writing-surface. The upper portion contained small drawers and a shelf on brass colonettes, or on lyre-shaped supports (Plate 78A).

The tall glass-fronted bookcase with a secretaire-drawer, and cupboard below, is a type of article which, because of its convenient arrangement and satisfying form. survived with few changes except in decorative detail for close on a hundred years from the days of Chippendale.

A delightful type of writing-desk, popular in drawing-rooms because of its compactness and ability to hold large quantities of material, is the Davenport. The term does not appear to have been much in use until the middle of the nineteenth century, although the type was in existence much earlier. The name is supposed to derive from a Captain Davenport, whose name appears in an account book of the firm of Gillow in the 1790's, as having been supplied with a desk, although no description of the piece is given.[2]

OTHER LIBRARY FURNITURE

A convenient invention was a table for storing rolled plans or charts. It was made in the form of a writing-table with imitation drawer-fronts, but the interior formed a deep space and was covered by a top divided into two flaps folding towards the centre. The form adopted by George Smith from Thomas Hope for

[1] See p. 56.
[2] Frank Davis in *Illustrated London News*, 26 March 1960.

the end-supports of writing-tables and deriving from one of Tatham's antique designs,[1] was found ideal for this type of furniture (Plate 77B).

Library steps for reaching high shelves were important and are found in various forms, some with a straight flight of steps with a newel-post in the form of a Tuscan column; others spiral, the steps set about a central post, as in the case of one delightful example made with the supports turned and painted to imitate bamboo (Plate 79A).

Small sets of steps were often made to fold into a table or stool. One especially successful production, an example of which is still in use at Trinity College, Oxford, was the 'Metamorphic Library Chair' made by those geniuses of mechanical furniture, Morgan & Sanders, and described in the *Repository* for 1811 as 'a novel and useful article'. The steps fold and are concealed under the seat, which is hinged at the front and is pulled forward to bring them into position (Plates 80A, 80B).

The revolving bookcase was a popular fitting in libraries, and was made in two chief forms. One consisted of several tiers of circular bookshelves on a table top supported by a pillar-and-claw, the other having a drum-shaped lower portion revolving on a concealed base, and also with tiers of bookshelves of diminishing size above (Plate 96). A circular and movable bookcase on the principle of the 'dumb-waiter' was described in the *Repository* for March 1810. Made by Morgan and Sanders, it had two shelves in the circular base, which was three feet in diameter, and five shelves in the upper stage. All of the latter were mounted on rollers and could be revolved independently in either direction. The effects of centrifugal force in the Regency age were no doubt as pronounced and disastrous as they are in our own day.

DINING-TABLES,
BREAKFAST, LOO AND DRAWING-ROOM TABLES

The characteristic dining-table of the Regency, of claw-and-pillar pattern, like the Trafalgar chair enjoys the honour of being among the most distinctive articles of furniture of that age, and more than any other type is associated with the traditional English dining-room. With its round-ended top and several leaves, enabling it to be extended or reduced in size as necessary, each leaf supported upon a central pillar carried on four curved legs, it is one of the most successful functional designs ever conceived, and in its cleanness and elegance one of the most beautiful

[1] See p. 56.

(Plate 86). The type was presumably not invented by Sheraton, although it par-
takes of the best qualities of his earlier refined style. He described in 1793 the
dining-table of this kind he had seen in the dining-parlour at Carlton House after
his visit to the Prince's establishment. 'In the middle are placed a large range of
dining tables, standing on pillars with four claws each, which is now the fashionable way of making these tables.' From then onwards the pillar-and-claw table
continued to be made for about forty years. In 1822 Peter Nicholson mentioned
in the Glossary of his work *The Practical Cabinet Maker* that pillar-and-claw tables
were still popular, and regarded as better than tables with frames and legs because
they did not interfere with the sitters at table.

Later variants, from about 1815 onwards, sometimes embodied octagonal
instead of turned pedestals, in accordance with the trend of the time, and tablet
or platform-bases instead of the claw type (Plate 87). George Smith encouraged
the use of the new sort by giving several designs which were intended to do
away with the splayed claw feet of the earlier Sheraton pattern, because, as he
believed, 'large projecting claws are a great inconvenience'. In place of claws he
used plinths, either resting directly upon the floor and of square plan with concave
sides, or, more commonly, of triangular form resting upon paw or ball feet.

In her novel *Emma*, published in 1816, Jane Austen described as 'modern' the
round table which took the place of the Pembroke-table 'upon which all Mr.
Woodhouse's meals had been crowded'. The type continued in popularity for
many years and is described in the *Repository* for July 1827, as convenient when it
was desired 'to avoid distinction in guests'. They were sometimes made extend-
able by the addition of segmental outer sections in the form of an outer border,
resting upon sliding bearers.

Circular tables were often known as breakfast-tables, and loo-tables, being
much used for that popular game. During the early Regency they were mostly of
pillar-and-claw type as described by Sheraton. Under Hope's influence they were
made with pedestals of triangular form (Plates 13, 73) and later more frequently
as a pillar rising from a circle of leaf-ornament, as drawn from classical originals
by Tatham. Tables of this last type seem to owe their origin to such articles as a
gueridon in mahogany, ebony and lemonwood, with lion-paw feet and palm-like
stem, made after classical models by Jacob in 1791, and which at one time belonged
to Joseph Bonaparte at Morfontaine.[1]

From about 1810 handsome circular or octagonal tables were used and known

[1] Illustrated in Lefuel, *Georges Jacob*, 1923, and mentioned by Watson in *Southill*.

as drawing-room tables, and they are among the distinctive forms of later Regency furniture (Plates 29, 31, 35). Numerous examples appear in the work of Smith, Brown and Nicholson. They embody delightful variations of design, especially in the decoration of the tops and in the form of the pedestals, much as in the case of library-tables. Brass-inlay was greatly favoured for decoration especially with rosewood and mahogany, and inlay of dark woods when timbers of lighter tone became more popular (see page 77). After about 1820 these tables became more elaborate and florid in character, and pedestals were often made in various turned and baluster shapes, sometimes of hexagonal and octagonal design.

Wine-tables are narrow and segmental in form, and were used to sit at while drinking wine before a fire after dinner. Two or more could be placed together to form a greater arc, accommodating a large party of men as, for example, after a college dinner.

The type of composite table of which Jane Austen writes in one of her letters[1] in 1800 was still in use, having been popular for about twenty years. Known as 'sets of dining tables', these consisted of three units each capable of being used separately. The centre portion had four legs, of which two swung out as gate-legs to support the large rectangular flaps. The end units were on four fixed legs, and had rectangular or D-shaped tops. The portions could be fixed together by means of brass clips, or, when not in use, dispersed as side-tables or smaller dining-tables. These as well as the pillar-and-claw styles could be made in different sizes, using varying numbers of separate units or pedestals. One of Gillow's composite tables, designed in 1795, was in ten sections and measured twenty-four feet. A variant of both types was patented by Richard Gillow in 1800 as an extending table formed by 'attaching to a table mounted upon a frame on legs, or a pillar and claws, wooden or metal sliders'. The table was extended by pulling out the sliders and laying leaves upon them. It was known as the Patent Imperial dining-table, and was sold under this name by several firms.

A table made by Gillow's to this patent in 1813 was described as 'set of imperial dining tables, 2 sets of 5 legs'. The legs were turned and reeded and with the table went a painted rack lined with baize to contain the leaves. This was supplied to Broughton Hall, Yorkshire for 50 guineas.[2] For the same house Gillow's supplied a 'set of tables consisting of 4 boards, each on a pillar, claw and castors' for £32 10s.

---

[1] J. E. Austen-Leigh, *A Memoir of Jane Austen*, 1870, p. 58.
[2] Hussey in *Country Life*, 14 April, 1950.

SIDEBOARDS, SIDE-TABLES AND DINING ACCESSORIES

The characteristic sideboard-table of the time of Adam and Hepplewhite, without drawers or cupboards but flanked by separate pedestals supporting knife-boxes or urns, continued in use during the early part of the Regency and is illustrated in Sheraton's *Cabinet Encyclopaedia* of 1804. Eventually the separate units were combined into a single massive piece of furniture with drawers beneath the centre part — a type which continued well into the Victorian era. In some smaller examples there were bow-fronts echoing the graceful lines of earlier Hepplewhite and Sheraton sideboards (Plate 83). The pedestals were often of tapering form, in many instances with the tops of the pedestals rising above the centre portion[1] (Plate 85). After about 1820 a high back-piece, often with a boldly carved central ornament, took the place of the elegant bronze rails of earlier sideboards (Plate 32B).

Sideboard-tables without drawers or pedestals varied little in their essential form, but there was an endless variety of designs for the supports, animal forms being especially popular (Plate 84), until about 1815, when scroll-shaped console supports deriving from Louis Quatorze models tended to become more common.[2]

The dumb-waiter with its tier of three or four shelves on a tripod base, was a useful appurtenance of the dining-room, and the pedestal supports were subject to variation in design much as in the case of sofa-tables, even lyre-shaped supports being sometimes used.

Running sideboards, 'sometimes vulgarly termed dinner waggons', as Smith remarked in his later work, were 'for the purpose of bringing the dinner at once to the dining-room. . . . In small families they answer the purpose of a dumb-waiter when the attendance of a footman is not required'.

Supper-canterburies, said by Sheraton to have been so named after their inventor, 'an archbishop of that see', and illustrated in the *Cabinet Dictionary*, were stands for plates and knives intended to be placed beside a table at supper.

Wine-coolers or wine-cisterns differ from cellarets in being intended, as the name indicates, to hold bottles surrounded by ice during a meal, whereas the cellaret is rather a storage place for wine in a dining-room. The former is lined

[1] See also pp. 85 & 113.   [2] See also p. 103.

with lead or zinc, sometimes fitted with a tap to draw off the melted ice, and was usable, as George Smith described in 1829, 'to receive the beer and ale jugs; at other times to ice the wine intended for use after dining.'

Wine-coolers or cisterns had no internal divisions and were usually, but not invariably, made without a lid. Some were in the favourite oval or oblong sarcophagus form with fluted sides, lion-mask drop-ring handles and lion-paw feet. Early examples made for modest households were in the form of shallow, open tubs of mahogany, bound with brass strips and standing on a claw base. A wine-cistern made by Gillow's in 1813 for Broughton Hall, Yorkshire[1] was shaped like a vase with gadrooned sides. The cost was 16 guineas.

Ice, by the way, played an important part in Regency dining and was stored in underground ice-houses which were sometimes two stories deep, where the ice was packed in straw. It was brought in the winter from the frozen rivers and lakes of the North, even from the Baltic.

Wine-cellarets or 'stores for wine' as Smith mentions, were lined with lead or zinc but with internal divisions to hold wine-bottles. The familiar oval or oblong sarcophagus shape was again the favourite pattern (Plates 32B, 84) but Richard Brown complained that cellarets or wine-coolers were often called sarcophagi when in fact they were not made in that form.

BEDS

Beds in the Regency period were of four main types: four-posters, canopy-beds, sofa-beds and tent-beds.

The best four-posters were usually of mahogany, the posts and cornices turned or carved in patterns derived from the design-books of Sheraton, George Smith and Michael Angelo Nicholson. Four-poster beds of fine quality were not as numerous in the Regency years as earlier, because great numbers had been made during the Hepplewhite period as a result of the revolutionary change in furnishing brought about by Robert Adam, and these beds were still serviceable in the early nineteenth century, and blended with Regency decorative schemes.

Canopy-beds were sometimes of the grandest quality, as in the case of the State Bed at Belvoir Castle* made for the visit of the Prince Regent in 1817. Canopy-beds were also made which aimed at a splendid appearance, usually to conform to a

[1] Hussey, op. cit.

special decorative scheme, such as Grecian, Etruscan, Chinese, Egyptian or Gothic, but with character of design taking precedence over quality of materials and workmanship. These beds were often made of beech or deal, rather than of the fine woods, and were painted (Plate 93). They do not survive in large numbers, partly because the number of houses where such special decorative schemes were used was comparatively small, partly because with various changes of fashion they went out of use and were broken up, and also because being made of softwoods they were more liable to attack from wood-beetle, especially in spare rooms which were not continually in use. Another reason is that during the later nineteenth century more modern notions of hygiene caused bed-hangings and wooden frames to be looked on with disfavour, and metal beds came more and more into use. Canopy beds of this type usually had their tops supported by attachments to the wall at the head, and by thin brass columns fixed into metal clamps at the feet. The woodwork was usually simple joinery, with a limited amount of carved or moulded decoration, the stylistic character being imparted mostly by means of painted or applied decoration.[1]

Both four-poster and canopy-beds had valances and curtains, and drapery more or less elaborate according to the wealth and style of the owner. The design-books of Sheraton, George Smith, Richard Brown and the Nicholsons were again fruitful sources of inspiration, as well as the designs appearing frequently in the *Repository of Arts*.

Sofa-beds were of two kinds, one being the French classical type with high ends of outward-curving scroll shape (Plate 92B). There was also the Louis Seize type depicted by Sheraton, after a model by Jacob, having square ends with slender corner-posts (Plate 92A). In the French manner both types stood sideways against the wall. These beds had a canopy hanging from a dome or crown, and more or less elaborately draped at the ends in the more splendid examples, or in the simpler types from a rod projecting outwards from the wall, and simply draped over the ends of the bed. There is a sofa-bed of the Sheraton type, but of about 1817, in the King's dressing-room at Belvoir. It has a small domed canopy above.

Tent-beds changed their form very little from the early years until the 1830's. Sheraton illustrates a folding camp-bed of this kind in the *Dictionary*. They had four corner-posts but lighter than for a four-poster bed, those at the feet being turned in patterns that varied with the taste of the period. The posts were joined not by an open cornice or tester but by a framework consisting of two curved rods

---

[1] See also pl. 93.

or stretchers from the head to the foot-posts, acting as a domed support for the drapery, which thus formed a tent. Tent-beds were considered more suitable for cottages, and for servants' and other small bedrooms. For villas and large houses four-poster beds were considered appropriate.[1]

Draperies were necessary for all types of beds in Regency times, from the richest State beds to that of the humblest servant, above all to secure privacy, especially as many bedrooms had no separate access, but were only reached by passing through other bedrooms. In the early Regency, satin, silk, damask and chintz were used for bed-draperies. Later, heavier materials such as velvet and merino came to be used, but at the end of the period lighter materials became popular again for hygienic reasons. In 1833 Loudon wrote, 'Chintz is generally preferred for bed-curtaining as it admits of being washed. Bed curtains, when of chintz, are generally lined with cotton of a different colour, sometimes plain and sometimes spotted. Dimity curtains, for both beds and windows, are considered in good taste, especially in the country, where they keep long clean.'

There were innumerable varieties of folding beds, camp and field-beds, and combined settee, couch, or cabinet-beds, mostly made by the firm of Morgan and Sanders, or by Messrs. Durham. These were probably very much in demand during the Napoleonic wars because of army and naval officers, sometimes with their wives, being compelled to move from one town to another. Press-beds, which lifted up vertically into a cupboard, were spoken of as being 'very common in kitchens, and, sometimes, in parlours where there is a deficiency of bedrooms'.

WARDROBES

The hanging press or cupboard replaced the tallboy or double chest of earlier times. Dwarf wardrobes, about 4 ft. 6 ins. high were popular, and were fitted with sliding trays of mahogany to hold clothing.

Some early wardrobes, of about 1808, were made similar to a break-front bookcase, but with solid doors and trays inside, and drawers below. In these early classical days it might have a simple pediment and triangular acroters, or corner-ornaments, which were sometimes called 'devil's-ears' by country servants who were fearful of heathen classical styles.

[1] Loudon.

In the later period there were greater variations of height and depth between the centre-portion and the wings, and pediments had the bold carving with classical ornament which was typical of this time (Plate 33B).

CHESTS-OF-DRAWERS

Early in the nineteenth century chests-of-drawers were of the Sheraton pattern, with reeded half-columns or pilasters at the front angles. They had either straight fronts or bow-fronts and a deep frieze above the top drawer (Plate 90A). The tall double chest-of-drawers of the mid-eighteenth century was out of favour, and George Smith made one design lower than usual to 'avoid the disagreeable alternative of getting on to chairs to place anything in the upper drawers'. Later in the Regency bow-fronts became even more popular, and colonnettes at the front angles were more prominent, and often reeded (Plate 90B). Their bases continued into turned and gadrooned feet in a fashion copied from Empire models. By 1826, as shown in George Smith's last book, the corner columns were completely detached, and rose from the thick slab-like plinth of the period. The columns had bold leaf-capitals and plain shafts. Dressing-commodes of this period, as they were sometimes called, were occasionally made with heavy foliated consoles instead of colonnettes at the sides.

DRESSING-TABLES

Early in the century men's dressing-tables were made of simple square form in the Sheraton tradition, the interior fitted up with compartments for the different toilet articles, and with a top opening out in two halves. When closed the top was flat and plain. This type continued to be popular at least until 1811, when Gillow's supplied one on square tapering legs to Broughton Hall.[1]

An exceptionally beautiful lady's dressing-table with a closing top on a pair of vase-shaped baluster supports expresses the manner in which a design for a sofa-writing table in the *Cabinet Encyclopaedia* of 1804 was adapted and refined in the execution (Plates 8A, 8B). Tatham's ubiquitous design of console end-supports deriving from a Roman table, which was adopted by Hope and Smith, was used for the dressing-table in the Victoria and Albert Museum (Plate 91).

[1] Hussey, op. cit., 14 April 1950.

By 1810 dressing-tables were being made more desk-like in shape with several drawers on either side, a central drawer and a kneehole below. The legs were simply turned and were joined by a tray-like platform stretcher. George Smith in 1828 showed toilet and dressing-tables having the glass fixed at the back between console supports, on the lines of more modern examples. One had end-supports of vase-shape like the sofa- and writing-tables of the time: another had curving crossed legs, like those of earlier years.

CHEVAL-GLASSES

Early in the century in the still-surviving Sheraton tradition cheval-glasses had slender turned frames with simple and beautiful working and were often surmounted by metal urn-finials. Others, in the spirit of Sheraton's later designs, had square framing of mahogany cross-banded with satinwood, also capped with metal finials, and set on bases with double-curved splay feet. In the later years the frames were often capped with pediments, heavily ornamented in the centre with scrolling or leaf-ornament. Occasionally cheval-glasses had standards headed with Egyptian or classical terminal figures.

Dressing-glasses, to stand on a chest-of-drawers or table, were sometimes like miniature cheval-glasses, but of horizontal form, and also in the form of a box-stand with small drawers having bone or ivory handles, and with turned upright supports. Occasionally the supports were in the form of lyres. For bedrooms with 'bamboo' furniture the supports of the dressing-glass would be turned with joints and painted in this fashion.

WALL-MIRRORS

The addiction to light and space in Regency times brought about the greatly increased use of wall-mirrors, which as Britton remarked were adopted 'to extend the apparent dimensions of our rooms'. Chimney-glasses, pier-glasses and great mirrors at the ends of rooms created those 'effects called the endless perspectives so much admired'[1] and which may be seen in the dining-room at Uppark,

[1] *Repository*, November 1818.

Sussex,* remodelled by Repton. In the early Regency such large glasses were mounted in fairly narrow mouldings of reeded, guilloche or coin-mould designs with paterae or square blocks at the corners, and often there was a cornice in the form of a *cavetto* moulding with gilt balls in the hollow, or shaped as a Grecian pediment with acroters. In later years the cornice or pediment became more elaborate with florid leaf ornament as shown in Smith's third book.

Among the most charming and characteristic productions of the late 1790's to about 1810 is the gilt overmantel-mirror in a classical frame. They are broad in proportion to their height, extending the full width of the fireplace, and usually have three glasses — a large centre one flanked by narrow upright ones (Plates 95A, 95B), though sometimes a single large glass is found, and other examples have a circular centre glass. The glasses are flanked with pilasters, or attached columns decorated with various classical motifs, and the cornice also is made in varying degrees of enrichment, but almost always includes a *cavetto* moulding with gilt, or sometimes black balls in the hollow. The spacing of the balls is close in the earlier models, wider in the later examples. The frieze is one of the most distinctive features of such mirrors. It is usually deep, containing a plaster relief of some mythological scene of votaries at a shrine, a triumphal car drawn by lions (Plate 95A), or a pastoral scene with children and musicians. Painted scenes of ships at sea or a romantic landscape are sometimes seen in the upper part, and glass panels were often used with a decoration painted on the back, or a design in black and gold in the *verre églomisé* process (Plate 95B).[1]

A similar type of mirror was made in a much smaller size with a single upright glass, but also with side pilasters, cornice moulding and a frieze panel containing a little painted landscape scene or classical decoration.

Circular convex mirrors are highly typical articles of Regency furnishing, and were popular from about 1795 to the 1820's. George Smith described them in 1808 as 'an elegant and useful ornament, reflecting objects in beautiful perspective on their convex surfaces; the frames, at the same time they form an elegant decoration on the walls, are calculated to support lights'. The circular frames of these mirrors were usually of the familiar *cavetto* form, with gilt balls in the hollow, and a black reeded slip between frame and glass. If this is missing the glass has probably been replaced in modern times. Many reproductions of these glasses have been made in the present century. In most of the glasses there is a cresting and underscrolling of acanthus leaves, often in the earlier specimens carved with

[1] See p. 136.

an exquisite degree of delicacy and fineness (Plate 94), but in later examples the foliage is more solidly and bluntly modelled. In many specimens the cresting is surmounted by the figure of an eagle, holding in his beak a festooned chain carrying balls. A charming use for these mirrors was to place them in the centre of the back wall of a sofa-alcove, especially if the walls were hung with drapery, the pleats radiating from the mirror.

Fig. 9. Lady Hamilton in a classical chair, by Francis Rehberg, 1794.

PROCESSES AND MATERIALS

FURNITURE-MAKING AND INDUSTRIALISM

It is commonly believed that woodworking machinery for furniture-making was generally in use during the Regency period, but there seems to be little or no evidence that this was so.

A comprehensive patent (No. 1951) for almost every possible kind of woodworking machinery had been granted to Sir Samuel Bentham in 1793. It covered planing, moulding, rebating, grooving, mortizing and sawing machinery, and was a remarkable inventive achievement in which almost all modern woodworking processes were anticipated. It appears, however, that Bentham's inventions were for many years confined to their use in convict prisons for cutting timber, and for making pulley-blocks for the Royal Navy.

Although many patents were registered for improved woodworking machines, there appears to be little evidence of their adoption for furniture-making during the Regency period.

Circular saws and straight-cutting mill-saws for heavy timber once driven by wind- or water-power, came to be driven by steam early in the nineteenth century. Lathes were probably the first machines to be elaborated during the Regency, judging by the more complicated character of turnery work during the 1820's, but the result of these improvements was a degeneration of style because of the difficulty of imposing restraint upon a machine.

It is significant that the volume entitled *The Circle of the Mechanical Arts*, published in 1813, although treating exhaustively of cabinet-making, among the other trades of the time, makes no mention of woodworking machinery other than Bentham's invention applied to pulley-block making, and to the use of steam-engines or water-mills for driving 'massive lathes' for 'very powerful works'. Martin suggests that manual power was more commonly used when he states, 'The common centre-lathe becomes a very powerful machine when worked by means of a large wheel turned by one or more labourers.'

In general it may be supposed that woodworking machinery was not in common use for furniture-making until the middle of the nineteenth century, because of the absence of any system for the industrial production of machine-tools. Up to this time most furniture-making was carried out by hand-tools, unquestionably so in small factories and country workshops.

In the larger workshops, factory methods were probably based on the increased separation of processes, a practice which had been developing since the mid-eighteenth century. Each craftsman was now responsible for an even more limited number of the commoner operations than formerly.

The restrained classical spirit of design, which favoured plain surfaces and straight lines must have greatly encouraged this kind of industrialization. There was a great reduction in the amount of carving and shaping that had to be done on the various portions of cabinet work, and cast metal ornaments were used in preference to carved decorations. Such features as the animal monopodium legs of furniture called for carving, but these details appeared only in the furniture of wealthier patrons, and for the less costly types of furniture the carved supports of cabinets and tables were of a square-section scroll-shaped kind which could easily be cut out with a bow-saw by semi-skilled labour.

Among the furniture-making firms of the Regency period the name of Gillow is by far the most famous and important, its reputation extending over the provinces as well as in London. The firm was founded in Lancaster by Robert Gillow in the early eighteenth century, and about 1765 premises were established in London on the site of the present showrooms of Waring and Gillow. In 1790 the firm was Robert Gillow & Co., Upholders, and in 1807 George and Richard Gillow & Co., merchants and cabinet-makers, etc. Richard Gillow, who died in 1811, did much to expand the business, and was the inventor of the improved dining-table patented in 1800, which was one of their most famous productions. His son Richard Thomas Gillow retired in 1830. The firm was one of the largest in the country, and its extensive records are preserved at the Victoria and Albert Museum. They form an invaluable guide to the furniture trade of the period.

Some features of design, for example voluted chair-backs, were adopted by them at an early date, but in other instances the more well-tried forms such as 'bobbin'-top table legs and folding-top dressing-tables were retained by them many years after their introduction. Many of their articles were branded, as is the gilt couch in the Victoria and Albert Museum.

VENEERING

Veneers were sheets of wood of especial richness of colour and figure of grain cut with special saws to extreme thinness, which were used by glueing to a base of more common wood. Not only large flat surfaces, such as the tops of tables, were veneered, but also shaped members like the underframing of tables, or brackets supporting shelves, to avoid the use of expensive solid wood. Veneers were not used solely, however, for the sake of economy, but to obtain rich effects with exotic woods of rich colouring and figure, which were extremely scarce, especially later in the Napoleonic wars when the difficulties of sea-borne trade made supplies uncertain. Special methods of cutting, also, enabled complex figures of grain to be obtained which could not economically be obtained from solid wood.

Almost all Regency furniture that was not painted or lacquered, with the exception of chairs and some dining-tables, was in fact veneered rather than made of solid wood. In the case of the finer pieces veneers displaying grain of rich colour and figure were used on a base of solid straight-grained mahogany. Among the woods used in the form of veneer for their beautiful colour or figuring of grain were figured mahogany and rosewood, and more exotic woods such as calamander wood and zebra wood.

INLAY AND BUHL-WORK

In the early Regency days inlay in the form of lines or stringings of rosewood (Plate 58), or cross-banding of satinwood or rosewood (Plate 59) were used on the light mahogany which was then favoured. In 1803 Thomas Sheraton was writing that 'crossbanding is now laid aside for the more durable work in solid brass'. This was often used in the form of thin brass beading in narrow strips round the edges of tables or marking out the lines of drawer fronts and table friezes.

From the same date onwards under the growing classical influence ebony and other dark woods were used in severe lines relieved perhaps by a restrained key-pattern motif in the corners, and by classical ornaments such as the honeysuckle and palmette at the end of friezes or marking the tops of table-legs. The lozenge-shaped ornaments that are often seen in the inlay of that period, especially round keyholes and drawer handles, derive from examples of the Directoire, when this design, which had been popular in the third quarter of the eighteenth century in France, was revived.

After about 1812 brass-inlay very largely supplanted wood-inlay (Plate 62). Strips of brass used for stringing lines became broader, and from about 1815 onwards more elaborate brass marquetry, or buhl-work became universal in good quality furniture.

Buhl-work properly consists of inlay in the manner practised by A. C. Boulle, cabinet-maker to Louis XIV, in which a design in thin sheet brass was set in a ground of tortoiseshell. In the original process the sheets of brass and tortoise-shell were clamped together between thin sheets of wood before cutting, and then cut out with a fine saw to the desired design. The two parts, *première-partie* and *contre-partie* were then in exact correspondence and the portion that formed the design in one part also served to form the background of another, and the two aspects of the design were often shown in a single piece of furniture, or in a pair of articles.

A similar method of working was adopted in the Regency examples of buhl-work, though wood veneer of rosewood or mahogany was used almost invariably instead of tortoiseshell. The use of tortoiseshell was usually confined to the very grandest pieces, or to small but important decorative devices, such as an inset panel containing the owner's arms or initials, and the tortoiseshell was sometimes backed by coloured metal, silver or gold foil.

Several distinct 'families' of brass-inlay work are discernible; in particular two main trends are obvious. One, an earlier phase, is for a simple decoration consisting of small, separate silhouette-like leaf and flower forms and simple classical and sometimes even 'Chinese' patterns arranged in isolated fashion (Plate 34A), perhaps in short chains of motifs (Plate 62), or in a large but open pattern of sparsely arranged details (Plate 63).

The second main class of brass-inlay consists of a more continuous type of decoration, covering the whole surface of the various features of a piece of furniture, such as the frieze, pilasters, door-panels, drawer-fronts or top of a table or cabinet. The later phase of buhl-work showed an increased tendency towards this 'all-over' treatment (Plates 34B, 36).

In this second phase the designs are in continuous and elaborate patterns with arabesques, broken curves and delicate *chinoiserie* motifs, deriving from the Louis Quatorze designs of Bérain and Boulle, or flowing acanthus scrolling reminiscent of the later neo-classic eighteenth-century *boulle* furniture. This type of work is usually found in the better quality and more imposing articles of furniture, though fine brass-inlay of running scroll-work was also used in smaller pieces such as sofa-tables of special richness. Often the two types of inlay are found in the same piece, the smaller detached motifs being used for the less important parts such as the under-framing of a table or piano-case or the side-panels of a cabinet.

This second main class of buhl-work also includes many articles of beautiful quality, in which the continuous designs are formed of leaf and flower shaped ornaments, more delicately and finely formed than the simple early examples. Sometimes small-scale separate motifs are joined in 'strip' form to make a continuous pattern. Designs such as these were not only executed but also probably originated by George Bullock (Plate 35).

From about 1812 onwards, when lighter woods came into greater favour, brass-inlay was often replaced by inlay of dark wood such as yew (see page 77).

CARVING

The craft of woodcarving decayed rapidly after the end of the eighteenth century. In *The Circle of the Mechanical Arts* published in 1813, T. Martin wrote: 'There are only eleven master carvers in London, and about sixty journeymen (though at one time there were six hundred). Many of the latter are now very old. They make no show of their work and live only in private houses. Carving in wood has long been in the background as a branch of the arts.' The *London Directory* of Pigot & Co., from 1823–4, lists twenty-three carvers and gilders, who were probably picture-frame and screen-makers. In the editions for 1832–3 the number had risen to sixty-three, no doubt because of the increased demand for carved foliate ornament instead of cast metal decoration, but comparatively few carvers were able to carry out the rich and sensitive designs of the Nicholsons. The tendency was towards the very bold carving of the simplified leaf forms which are more common at the end of the Regency age, and which often has the appearance of being intended to be cast in iron rather than executed in wood. In fact, the increased demand for bold ornament in the 1820's caused motifs to be made in *papier-mâché*, a material used in the eighteenth century, which very largely replaced the composition ornaments of whiting and size which had been in use during the Adam period. The *papier-mâché* ornaments could be finished by carving, quite deep undercutting being possible, and such articles as lion masks and paterae were produced in this material.[1]

METALWORK

Most metalwork for furniture was cast in brass, or more rarely in bronze. In the case of such articles as door or drawer-knobs the centre part was cast solid, and the plate and knob itself cast of such thin metal that it was 'no thicker than a shilling'.[2]

Great differences of quality are discernible, not only in the character of the design of metal ornaments, but in the degree of hand finishing given. Many of the metal workers in England during the Regency were French craftsmen who had fled their country at the Revolution, and it was acknowledged that 'The French excel in chasing, as their numerous small ornaments used in decoration . . . fully demonstrate'.

The dangerous methods of gilding metal employing mercury, which had been in use from earlier times, continued until late in the nineteenth century. In these processes an amalgam of six or eight parts of mercury to one of gold was applied to the metal. The object was then subjected to heat in a furnace to drive off the mercury, leaving the gold deposited on the surface. In the final burnishing process various substances such as beeswax, red ochre, verdigris, copper scales, alum, vitriol and borax were used to heighten the colour of the gilding, and heat was again applied, but the process was a highly dangerous one because of the extremely poisonous nature of the fumes of mercury given off in the firing. Other, and less dangerous methods of gilding metals were used especially in this country. These involved coating the metal with solutions of chloride of gold in ether, or of gold in aqua-regia and similar solutions. In the latter half of the eighteenth century Matthew Boulton had evolved a safe method of gilding which produced excellent results. The term 'ormolu' for gilded metal derives from the fact that the gold (French *or*) was ground (*moulu*) to a fine powder to enable it to amalgamate more completely with the mercury. A great deal of so-called 'English Ormolu' was lacquered brass, without any coating of gold, but frequently brass and gilded ornaments are found together in a single piece of furniture.

[1] Therle Hughes in *Antiques Review*, No. 2, 1949.   [2] Martin, *The Circle of the Mechanical Arts*, 1813.

LACQUER WORK

With the revival of *chinoiserie* at the beginning of the nineteenth century there was a renewal of interest in oriental lacquer, which had first been popular in England during the reign of Charles II. The art of lacquering was based on the sap of the lacquer tree *Rhus vernicifera*, known as *Chi-shu* by the Chinese. The lacquer gum was produced by making incisions in the bark of the tree and collecting the fluid, which was at first thick and greyish. It was strained through a cloth, simmered over a fire to remove impurities, and kept in stoppered vessels. In use the lacquer gum was combined with various pigments to obtain the desired final colour. Upon drying it hardened into the sought-after glossy surface.

The essence of perfect lacquer work was in the patience and skill devoted to building up a thick and lustrous surface. For work of the best quality ten to fourteen coats were given, but it was said that as many as twenty or more coats were sometimes used. The parts intended to be in relief were built up with a paste of clay, and afterwards painted.

Although oriental lacquer was either Chinese or Japanese, it was often referred to indiscriminately as 'India' work or 'Japan'. It was difficult to classify the origin of any lacquer because little of it was sold in the place of its origin, but was sent to one of the great trading centres such as the Coromandel coast, Dutch Batavia, or the port of Canton, before being bought by European merchants.

The Japanese became adept at lacquer work very early, and in the fifteenth century even Chinese craftsmen were sent to Japan to learn the finest secrets of the art. The Emperor K'ang-Hsi (1662–1722) attributed the greater success of the Japanese to the damper climate of that country, which caused the lacquer to dry more slowly, and consequently harder, thus helping to ensure a more perfect result.

Chinese lacquer may usually be identified by the robust and light-hearted quality of the designs, which abound in human figures. Some forms of Chinese lacquer are decorated with inset pieces of mother-of-pearl (*lac burgauté*), ivory, jade and semi-precious stones.

Japanese lacquer is usually painted in lower relief than Chinese, the surface often has a richer gloss, and the designs are rarely peopled with figures. Apart from the scenic panels, the surrounding frames, sides and shelves of a cabinet were often decorated with an all-over pattern of trailing vine-leaves and berries, the shapes of the leaves being repeated with mathematical exactitude, as though first marked on the surface with a stamp.

Probably the greater part of the oriental lacquer bought in Regency days was Japanese. Panels of this lacquer were made up into cabinets by English craftsmen in the accepted style of the day, sometimes with gilded colonettes at the corners, and paw-feet of ormolu or gilded brass (Plates 24A, 25).

JAPANNING

Japanning is the term properly applied to English lacquer work. In the *Artist's Assistant* of 1801, it was 'understood as the art of covering bodies by grounds of opake colours in varnish, which may be either afterwards decorated by paintings, or left in a plain state'.

Japanning embraces not only the work of the finest craftsmen, but also medium quality commercial work, mostly consisting of small occasional articles of furniture, as well as domestic work performed as an elegant amusement for young ladies.

The work of japanning was fully described in a number of manuals, the earliest and most important of which was the famous work by John Stalker and George Parker published in 1688, the *Treatise of Japanning and Varnishing, Being a compleat Discovering of those Arts. With the best way of making all sorts of Varnish for Japan. . . .* Another useful work was *The Ladies Amusement, or Whole Art of Japanning Made Easy*, containing over 1,500 motifs, including some designs by Pillement, published about 1758 and, later in the century, Robert Sayer's *New Chinese Drawing Book*, published at his shop in Fleet Street, London.

The oriental motifs shown included figures, trees, rocks, bridges, pagodas, temples, pavilions and a host of other devices. Many of the designs are engagingly naïve, unpractical and fanciful, especially those of architectural character, which often appear a little precarious, but this tendency adds greatly to the likability of many of the articles produced and it is one of the means by which English japanning, which at its best is sometimes difficult to distinguish from Chinese lacquer, may be identified (Plate 24B).

The process of japanning differed fundamentally from oriental work in that the substance used was not the true lacquer, but gum-lac, seed-lac or shellac. These are various forms of a resinous substance secreted from certain trees when they have been attacked by the insect *Coccus lacca*. It is produced in Bengal, Burma,

Assam and Siam, and is used in the manufacture of various varnishes, French polish and sealing wax.

In japanning a clear varnish was used, and made black or given any colour desired by means of opaque colours, particularly lamp-black, crimson lake and vermilion, Indian red, white lead, ochre, and flake white. The scarlet and green japanning of the late seventeenth and eighteenth centuries were now supplanted in favour almost entirely by black Japan, though metal dusts, such as gold and bronze powder, and finely ground glass, were used to give a glittering speckled effect of gold or silver on a ground of red or yellow, especially for the framing of lacquer panels.

A number of small articles such as cabinets and workboxes were made in ivory Japan, and music-stands in scarlet.

An important difference between the more popular products and the finer work of the craftsmen was in the slighter relief given to the designs in the cheaper commercial and domestic examples, but chiefly the difference lay in the number of coats of lacquer applied and in the care taken in building up the surface. Instead of the ten or more coats used in the finest productions, each carefully rubbed down before the next was applied, only one or two coats of ground colour were used, and the result is that to-day much of this commercial japanned work has a dry and starved appearance. There was only a small depth of relief, if any, and the designs were painted with bronze powder in oil instead of being carried out in gold leaf.

In Regency days there was probably very much less japanning as a domestic amusement than in the early and middle eighteenth century, when it was a general craze. Most of the popular articles of japanned work were sold not in the show-rooms of the cabinet-makers as much as in circulating libraries and fancy-work shops specializing in the sale of small articles and souvenirs, such as 'The Temple of Fancy' at Rathbone Place, London.

However, these unpretentious specimens of japanned furniture have a great deal of charm, and their designs often possess pleasing *naïveté*, which makes them now as in Regency days, delightful objects for informal domestic interiors.

PAINTED FURNITURE

A great deal of furniture in Regency times was painted, especially the large class of articles known as Fancy Furniture, consisting of small bookshelves, work-tables and similar occasional articles (Plate 67B). A great deal of bedroom furniture also, such as chests-of-drawers, dressing-tables, washing-stands and wardrobes were made of beech, pine, deal and other cheap woods and painted (Plate 27).

Painted furniture was used extensively in the smaller houses, and even in larger ones articles of better quality such as drawing-room chairs were often painted and gilt, and inexpensive dining-room chairs and stools, especially Trafalgar chairs and similar articles in strict Grecian taste, were painted, frequently black, or green in imitation of bronze (Plate 39A).

In January 1809 the *Repository* commented, 'Bronze still prevails as a groundwork for chairs, sofas, cabinets, &c., and will always be classic when delicately and sparingly assisted with gold ornaments' (Plates 22B, 20B, 77B). In April of the same year we are informed: 'Black chairs, ornamented with metal gilt in various elegant devices, are in universal use, and certainly have a good effect from their great neatness; and there is hardly any apartment in which they may not be suitably placed.' By August 1814 the *Repository* was remarking, of some designs for chairs, that they 'may be stained black, or as the present taste is, veined with vitriol, stained with logwood, and polished to imitate rosewood'.[1]

Articles in the strict classical taste of Thomas Hope were often painted with classical ornaments such as honeysuckle and palm, trailing leaf-designs, or classical scenes copied from 'Etruscan' vases (Plates 12B, 38A, 55, 96).

Although much painted furniture was made of cheap wood, painting was not invariably resorted to merely for the sake of cheapness, but rather to create a special decorative scheme, as in the case of much of George Smith's designs. Thus articles in any of the distinctive tastes were frequently painted, and occasionally when of better quality might even be made of mahogany. Such pieces in the Etruscan taste as large china-cabinets were painted in the colours of an Etruscan vase with Grecian ornament in very dark brown or terracotta red. Graining and painted marbling were used, especially for such things as cabinet and table tops.

Designs for painted ornaments, such as classical figures, Greek honeysuckle, palm, lotus, poppies, cornucopias, and fret or key patterns for borders, were published in Ackermann's *Repository* and could also be bought at circulating libraries and stationers' shops. They were used for decorating small articles of furniture, such as sofa- and writing-tables, in black pen-work in a panel or border

[1] See also p. 93.

of light-coloured wood with the surrounding wood stained black (Plates 60, 61). A large commode in the Victoria and Albert Museum is decorated in this manner.

A host of minor articles were sold at stationers' shops and circulating libraries, and at special establishments such as 'The Temple of Fancy' at 34 Rathbone Place, London, owned by S. J. Fuller, where could be found, as we are told in the *Repository* for January 1822, 'an extensive collection of handsome screens, both Plain and Ornamented, Screen-Poles, elegant Stands for Table-Tops and Chess-Boards, Card-Racks, Flower Ornaments, and White-Wood Boxes, in a variety of shapes, for painting the inlaid Ebony and Ivory, with every requisite useful for Painting and Ornamenting the same.'

In the late Regency period the vogue began for large decorations of flowers, painted naturalistically in rich colours on a paper base in pieces of furniture such as drawing-room commodes. The beginnings of this fashion, which continued into Victorian times, are seen in the large panels of realistically painted flowers in drawing-room commodes by Jacob-Desmalter[1] towards the end of the restoration in France. The borders of semi-formal ornament surrounding the flower-paintings often embody Louis Quatorze motifs (Plate 37).

The splendid late Regency commode illustrated (Plate 55) has panels painted with figures of dancing bacchantes and smaller still-life groups from the decorations at Herculaneum, published in *Le Antichita d'Ercolano* at Naples in 1757.

UNDER-GLASS PAINTING AND VERRE-ÉGLOMISÉ

Decorative glass panels, painted with ornaments or with landscapes and figures in various colours or in gold and black, are sometimes found in various articles of Regency furniture, especially gilt mirrors (Plate 95B), and barometers, and more rarely as plaques in cabinets and writing-desks.

The term *verre-églomisé* is often applied to all kinds of this work, but it should properly be used only for the type of decoration carried out in gold-leaf applied to the under-side of the glass and engraved with a design. The backgrounds of the designs were executed frequently in black, but also in other colours, particularly in blue, white and maroon in the early nineteenth century examples. A design applied to a glass panel by means of brush and paint is not true *verre-églomisé*, but under-glass painting. The two processes, however, were sometimes combined

[1] Nicolay.

in a single example, a *verre-églomisé* design in gold and black being surrounded by under-glass painting in various colours. *Verre-églomisé* designs were nearly always abstract or formal decorative motifs, whereas under-glass painting often depicted landscape scenes and figures, as well as flower motifs. The technique was known in ancient Alexandria and Italy, and examples have been found in the Catacombs. It was practised throughout the Middle Ages and achieved its greatest popularity at the end of the eighteenth century and the beginning of the nineteenth, when many designs from painted decorations at Pompeii and Herculaneum were produced in this manner.

The name of the process derives from J. B. Glomy, a well-known art-dealer of Paris who died in 1786. He revived and popularized the technique, and his name was applied to it by the French archaeologist Carrand about 1825.[1]

POLISHING

French polishing was introduced into this country after the peace of 1814. Hitherto furniture had been polished with beeswax and turpentine, and linseed oil also was often used. Sheraton describes in his *Dictionary* the use of linseed oil and brickdust, which formed 'a kind of putty' under the rubbing cloth, by which means a fine polish was 'infallibly' produced. When the new polish was introduced many people had their furniture stripped and re-polished, sometimes with regrettable results.

The original French polishing process was much more elaborate than the methods known by the name at the present day. Several different varieties of lac were used, dissolved in spirits of wine, but the principle secret of success lay in the amount of time and skill that were devoted, firstly to the patient building-up of a surface by continuous rubbing with a pad of cloth in a circular movement, and then to the 'spiriting-off' stages, in which less and less polish was used, and increasing proportions of spirit, until a perfect gloss was obtained. Modern French polishing consists in the use of little more than ordinary shellac in turpentine, and the tendency is to create a thick film of polish rather than the thin lustrous surface given by the early process.

[1] *Connaissance des Arts*, August 1957.

METHOD OF MAKING AND USING THE FRENCH POLISH
From Richard Brown, *The Rudiments of Drawing*
Cabinet and Upholstery Furniture, 1820

Take of mastic one ounce, sandarac one ounce, seed lac one ounce, shell lac one ounce, gum lac one ounce, gum arabic one ounce, and virgin wax quarter of an ounce; these reduce to powder, and put into a bottle with a quart of rectified spirits of wine: after standing some hours, it will be fit for use.

Application   Make a ball of cloth, and on it occasionally put a little of the polish: afterwards wrap over the ball a piece of calico, which touch on the outside with a little linseed oil; then rub the furniture hard, with a circular motion, until a gloss is produced; finish with one third of the polish to two thirds of the spirit of wine.

Another method of making the French Polish is, to put into a glass bottle one ounce of gum lac, two drams of mastic in drops, four drams of sandarac, three ounces of shell lac, and half an ounce of gum dragon: the whole being reduced to powder, add to it a piece of camphor, the size of a nut, then pour on it eight ounces of rectified spirit of wine; afterwards stop the bottle close, which put near a gentle fire, or on a German stove. The bottle must not be more than half full at the time of dissolving the gum, and the solution should be made in hot sand, for fear of catching fire. The first method is by far the best, and is unattended with danger.

PRINCIPAL CABINET-MAKING WOODS

Amaranth: See *Purplewood*

Amboyna: From West Indies. Warm, light brown with a small 'bird's eye' figure. Used for complete surfaces and also for banding. Often confused with thuya wood (Plates 35, 63, 64).

Ash: Whitish or light brown, sometimes tinged with pink. Straight grain, but coarse uneven texture. Used for Windsor chairs and drawer linings, and in pollarded form for veneers.

Beech: Whitish or light brown, with tiny flecks of brown. Harder than deal, but softer than mahogany, and very subject to attacks of wood-beetle. Used for carcase work and framing, and especially during the Regency for painted chairs.

Birch: Yellow, with very faint, straight grain, and even texture. Used in chair-making and as a substitute for satinwood.

Boxwood (Buxus sempervirens): From Europe and Asia Minor. Yellow, and without markings, very hard and heavy. Used for stringing lines and borders on satin-wood, and for small objects such as boxes, knobs, turned articles and parts of musical instruments.

Calamander: From Ceylon. Often wrongly called 'Coromandel' wood. Yellowish brown, with black mottling and streaks. Used as a veneer and for bandings.

Cedar (Cedrus atlanticus and Cedrus libani): A reddish-brown soft wood of straight grain, used for the interiors of chests and wardrobes and for drawer-linings because of its aromatic properties, which cause it to repel moths.

Chestnut: Light greyish-brown hard wood, closely resembling oak, but with a more pronounced figure. Used for carcase-work and frames, especially for pieces in oak, and also in veneer form as a substitute for satinwood.

Coromandel Wood: From the Coromandel coast of India. Resembles Calamander wood. Black with yellowish streaks. Used as a veneer (Plates 34A, 50A).

Ebony: From Ceylon and East India. One of the heaviest woods, very black and hard, close-grained. Used as an inlay, and in French furniture for cabinets in the late eighteenth century, and also in England in the Louis Quatorze revival, but substitutes such as pear-wood stained black were then more frequently used (Plate 2A).

Elm: English. Light brown. Irregular grain and coarse texture. Often used for seats of Windsor chairs, but rarely otherwise in Regency furniture except as veneer in the cross-sawn form: i.e. 'burr-elm' or 'pollarded elm'.

Harewood: Sycamore veneer, stained green or greyish. Popular for inlays and bandings in the eighteenth century. Also known as 'silverwood'.

Holly: White or greyish, fine-grained and hard. Used as an inlay and in marquetry furniture and small fancy articles, frequently stained.

Kingwood (Dalbergia ciarensis): From Brazil. Light yellowish-brown, with strongly contrasted darker streaks, regularly spaced. Known in eighteenth century as 'prince's wood' and used as a veneer. Later used for cross-banding (Plates 30, 85).

Mahogany, Honduras (Swietenia macrophylla): From Jamaica, Columbia, Guatemala, Haiti, San Domingo and Yucatan. Also called Central American mahogany, or Baywood. Came into use in the latter half of the eighteenth century. Reddish brown with slightly darker brown streaks, and often showing white in the grain. Lighter and browner in colour, and more straight-grained than Spanish mahogany (Plates 59, 62).

Mahogany, Spanish (Swietenia mahogani): Also called West Indian or Cuban mahogany. Richer in colour, being more reddish than Honduras mahogany, and often more highly figured. First used in England early in the eighteenth century, but very scarce after 1800.

'Fiddle-Back' Mahogany: Used in form of veneers for decorative panels in highest quality articles. It is cut where branches or roots join the trunk, as is also 'mottle' and 'curl' mahogany (Plate 77B).

Maple: Many varieties in N. Europe and N. America. Pale whitish- or greyish-brown, the grain straight but not prominent. Often used as a veneer and for picture-frames, especially in the 'bird's-eye', cross-sawn variety.

Oak: English. Little used for cabinet furniture except for pieces in Gothic style, and for carcase-work, such as drawers and cabinet frames. Straight-grained when straight-sawn, but showing beautiful medullary rays or light figure when 'quarter-sawn', and 'bird's-eye' curls when pollarded (Plate 73).

Partridge-Wood (Andera inermis): From Brazil. Also known as Anderlin, and pheasant-wood. A heavy, straight-grained wood of coarse, uneven texture. Light or reddish brown with dark brown feather markings like a partridge or pheasant.

Pear: Light reddish or yellowish brown, hard and fine-textured. Used as an inlay and in chair-making.

Purplewood (Peltogyne pubescens): From Guiana and Brazil. Also called Purpleheart, Violetwood, and Amaranth. Purple when first cut, turning to brown on exposure, and then resembling rosewood. Fine, hard and even-textured. Used as a veneer and for bandings.

Rosewood (Fr. Palissandre) (Dalbergia): From Brazil. Reddish brown with dark brown or black streaks. Used as a veneer, and for small parts and articles such as caskets, knobs and buttons (Plates 52B, 66B, 68, 74, 77A).

Satinwood, West Indian (Xanthoseylium flavium): From Brazil and Guiana. Came into use about 1760. Pale to deep yellow. Fine grain, sometimes richly figured (Plates 65, 72, 90A).

Satinwood, East Indian (Chloroseylon swietenia): From Ceylon. Introduced into England about 1780. Pale or golden-yellow. Used as a veneer and for inlay, and in the solid for small articles.

Snakewood (Piratinera guinanensis): From British Guiana. The heaviest known wood.

Blackish and reddish brown, with dark red and brown spots and snake-like markings. Used as a veneer.

Sycamore: White and fine-grained. Used for inlay and as a veneer, often stained as a substitute for satinwood, or when stained green, known as 'harewood'.

Thuya-Wood: From Africa. Rich, golden-brown with small 'bird's-eye' figure. Used as a veneer.

Tulip-Wood (Fr. *Bois de rose*) (*Dalbergia frutescens tomentosa*): From Brazil. Reddish yellow, with carmine streaks. Fades when exposed. Not to be confused with rosewood.

Yew: English. A fairly open-grained hard wood, reddish brown in colour. Used for small articles such as boxes and caskets, and in the backs of Windsor chairs, and other turned articles: also in form of burr veneers.

Zebra-Wood (*Pithecolobium racemiflorum*): From Guiana. It is a heavy wood, of light brown colour, close-grained, with streaks of much darker brown. Chiefly used as a veneer.

WOODS CLASSIFIED BY GRAIN AND FIGURE

Plain woods

Ash, Beech, Birch, Box, Cedar, Chestnut, Ebony, Elm, Harewood, Holly, Mahogany, Maple, Oak, Satinwood, Sycamore.

Streaky-grain woods

Calamander, Coromandel, Kingwood, Partridge-wood, Purplewood, Rosewood, Snakewood, Tulipwood, Yew, Zebra wood.

'Bird's eye' or burr-grain and pollarded woods

Amboyna, Elm, Maple, Oak, Thuya-wood, Yew.

Pollarded woods, usually oak and elm, are cut across the trunk near the roots, where the grain is formed into tight little 'bird's eye' curls.

SHORT GLOSSARY OF UNUSUAL TERMS

Acroters: Triangular-shaped ornaments at the upper corners of cabinets, bookcases, cupboards, etc. Originally statue-platforms on Greek buildings.

Anthemion: A form of ornament related to the honeysuckle flower. Properly applied to a frieze in which honeysuckle alternates with palmette ornament. (q.v.)

Caryatid: A support for a table or cabinet, etc., in the form of a female sculptured figure.

Colonnettes: Slender column-shaped supports, with turned or carved ornaments.

Console: A bracket or support in the form of a scroll.

Frieze: A horizontal band or border beneath a table-top, or under the cornice of a cabinet or cupboard.

Gadrooning: A form of ornament consisting of a series of short convex ribs, or concave flutes, sometimes twisted in S-form. Also called nulling or loging.

Guilloche: A form of ornament used for borders, friezes, etc., consisting of a series of interlaced circles or ovals.

Monopodium (Pl. monopodia): Supports for tables or other articles, in the shape of animals (lions or chimeras) having the head and body formed with a single leg and foot.

Palmette: A form of ornament similar to the honeysuckle. A conventional form of palm-leaf.

Patera: A flat circular or oval ornament, usually applied or carved, but sometimes painted.

Pediment: A classical feature, usually triangular, like a shallow gable-end, surmounting the tops of bookcases, cabinets, cupboards, etc.

Pilaster: A support shaped as a flat column applied to the front of a cabinet, etc.

Rosettes: Raised circular ornaments with flower decoration.

Terms, or terminal figures: Supports or pedestals shaped as figures with natural heads, busts and feet, and with the legs and lower bodies formed as tapering columns.

Volutes: Spiral-shaped ornaments, used in the capitals of Ionic columns and in chair-backs, etc.

APPENDIX

Entries from the catalogue of the sale of 'Old English and other furniture from Deepdene, Dorking, Wednesday, July 18th, 1917', relating to all items in the sale which are illustrated in Thomas Hope's *Household Furniture and Interior Decoration*, 1807

Note: The first plate numbers given refer to the plates in Hope's *Household Furniture*. Plate numbers in square brackets refer to illustrations in the present work.

ENGLISH FURNITURE, CHIEFLY OF THE EMPIRE PERIOD

Lot No.

293. A pair of Empire gilt settees carved with rams' heads and honeysuckle ornament, the seats covered with green velvet.

3 ft. 9 in. wide. Plate 22

297. An Empire circular table, the top of rosewood, inlaid with tulips in brass, on gilt tripod stand carved with leopards' heads.

24 in. diam. Plate 32

298. An Empire circular mahogany table, the top inlaid with star ornament, and a wreath of foliage in ebony and silver, on triangular stand with black claw feet.

42 in diam. Plate 39

[Plate 13]

300. A pair of Empire fire screens of mahogany, with bronze appliques, and inlaid with stars in brass, surmounted by bronze figures of Sphinxes.

4 ft. 9 in. high. Plate 28

301. A pair of Georgian mahogany wine coolers, of Classical form, carved with masks.

38 in. wide. Plate 24

302. Pair of Empire X-shaped arm-chairs, with black framework carved with flutings, the seats and backs stuffed and covered with yellow silk brocade.

Plate 20

304. A pair of Empire X-shaped mahogany seats, carved with leopards' heads and claws.

28 in. wide. Plate 12

306. A Suite of Empire Furniture, black and gold, carved with Classical ornament, and mounted with bronze Egyptian figures, animals, etc., the seats stuffed and covered with yellow silk brocade, consisting of:

Two oblong seats, 5 ft. 6 in. wide.
Four arm-chairs.

Plates 8, 17 & 46
[Plate 21]

Fig. 10. Classical meditation, by Henry Moses, 1823.

NOTES

1. (p. 30) The attribution to Henry Holland is an early one, and has been followed by many writers, in fact at one time by myself in *Royal Pavilion: an Episode in the Romantic*, 1959.

2. (p. 31) The two original pier-tables were copied by the English firm of Bailey and Saunders about 1819 to make two pairs, and thus to provide for a more balanced arrangement in the final furnishing of the Royal Pavilion at Brighton, where they were still being used (see G. de Bellaigue, *Buckingham Palace*, 1969). The ormolu work on the English copies is distinctly inferior to the French originals.

 The author's attribution to Weisweiler was challenged by Miss Dorothy Stroud in her admirable work *Henry Holland, His Life and Architecture*, 1966 (p. 81). Following more recent investigations the conclusion has been reached that the two original tables are most probably of French manufacture (G. de Bellaigue, loc. cit., and the *Burlington Magazine*, September 1967). More recently it was discovered by Mr. de Bellaigue that the top of one of the original tables had been levelled with the aid of some pieces of French playing cards.

 I am greatly indebted to Mr. Francis J. B. Watson for concurring in the suggestion that the Carlton House pier-tables, now at Buckingham Palace, are French, and almost certainly the work of Weisweiler.

 Mr. Watson states that after dismantling and closely examining one of them he has 'no doubt whatever that it is French. Every point of the construction suggests that, and is totally different from the way an English cabinet-maker would have built the piece . . . I should say, therefore, there is little doubt that these pieces were supplied to Holland's order (but not to his design, I should suppose) by Daguerre . . . I think there is a very real probability that the tables are by Weisweiler.'

The two original pier-tables in the Royal Collection closely resemble a pair attributed to Weisweiler which were included in the exhibition 'Orfevrerie de Portugal' held at the Musée des Arts Decoratifs in the Louvre in 1954, and illustrated in *Styles de France: objets et collections*, Paris, 1955. The style, construction and particularly the ormolu work with its lozenge-shaped motifs and 'spider-web' design are identical in character to the Royal pier-tables.

3. (p. 31)   The fireplace, with its Chinese terminal figures in ormolu of the same character as those of the pier-tables must also be assumed to be French, but the snake-entwined chairs were made in London by the French emigré craftsman François Hervé (see G. de Bellaigue, *Burlington Magazine*, September, 1967).

4. (p. 33)   In Mr. John Harris's *Regency Furniture Designs, 1803–1826*, 1961, are reproduced two drawings in the Pierpont Morgan Library, stated to be from the hand of Henry Holland. They represent pier-tables intended for the architect's own house in Sloane Place, and for Carlton House, and clearly show the influence of Weisweiler.

5. (p. 33)   Mr. F. J. B. Watson's comprehensive monograph *Louis XVI Furniture*, 1960, amply describes and illustrates the French antecedents of English Regency furniture in that reign.

6. (p. 34)   The 'Etruscan' style of the late eighteenth and early nineteenth centuries derived from the works of art which were supposed to be remains of the Etruscans, forerunners of the Romans, who had lived between the Arno and the Tiber, from the eighth to the first centuries B.C. Most of the sculptures excavated were truly Etruscan, but the so-called 'Etruscan' vases, the paintings upon which provided material for so much Regency decoration and furniture design, were in fact late Greek, especially the red-figured pottery of the fifth century. The wall-paintings of the Etruscan tombs were also strongly affected by Greek art.

7. (p. 35)   The question arises as to whether Charles Tatham might not have had a hand in the design of the earlier pieces at Southill embodying French character, but there is no record that he ever visited Paris. He is more likely to have been responsible for the design of the later pieces, especially those supplied by the firm in which his own brother was a partner.

8. (p. 41)   This personage was a member of the Kinska family, whose rococo palace in Prague still exists. The *Pavillon Chinois* was on one of the Princess's Bohemian estates (Lefuel, *Georges Jacob*).

9. (p. 43)   The only other known work of this craftsman is a fine pair of candelabra at the Bowes Museum*, Barnard Castle, Co. Durham.

10. (p. 46)   The first collection had been bought by the nation for the British Museum. Hope's purchase was in fact only half of the second collection. The other half was lost at sea while being brought to England.

11. (p. 46)   General Clark had married Sir William Hamilton's sister, the Dowager Countess of Warwick.

12. (p. 48)   The circular table made to Hope's design (Plate 13), which is now in the Victoria and Albert Museum, is believed to have been at Deepdene. Indeed, a table of this kind is shown in a drawing dated 1825 by W. H. Bartlett of an interior there, and a description of it appears in the sale catalogue of 18 July 1917 (see page 143). More than one example of this design is known to exist, however: one was in a Paris showroom at the time of writing.

   The Bartlett drawing of Deepdene is contained in a volume of drawings, including views of the Deepdene Estate with some architectural sketches of the house, by W. H. Bartlett and Henry Williams, which was sold at Sotheby's on 25 May 1960. No other articles of Thomas Hope furniture appear in these Deepdene drawings.

13. (p. 54)   Little seems to be known of the life of this cabinet-maker who in 1828 referred to his forty years experience in the trade. He was then living at 40 Brewer Street, and he may have been the father of George Smith Junior, a topographical draughtsman who lived at 41 Brewer Street, and exhibited at the Royal Academy in 1819. The elder Smith must not be confused with the George Smith, architect (1783–1869), who was Surveyor to the Mercer's Company, and designed important buildings in London.

14. (p. 55)   Some drawings by J.-L. David, in the collection of Mr. F. J. B. Watson, show vigorous and naturalistic animal forms such as dogs' heads and suggest that the French designer might have been the source of Smith's inspiration, as of many other innovations.

15. (p. 61) This copy of Denon, bearing Henry Holland's signature on the fly-leaf, was in the collection of the late Sir Albert Richardson.

16. (p. 61) *Chimera.* A fabulous animal of classical mythology, having the head of a lion, the body of a wild she-goat, and the tail of a dragon.

    Griffin or Gryphon. A fabulous creature having the head and wings of an eagle and the body of a lion.

    Sphinx. In Greek mythology, the winged monster of Thebes, with a woman's head and breast, and a lion's body. In Egyptian antiquity a figure with a lion's body and the head of a woman or man.

    In Regency days a certain amount of fantasy was indulged from time to time in transposing the various zoological features of legendary animals in different ways.

17. (p. 65) The earliest known intimations of the Chinese spirit at the Pavilion, antedating the famous gift of Chinese wall-papers to the Prince in 1802, appear in a drawing by Holland in the Royal Library at Windsor, dated July 1801. This embodies a Chinese exterior, somewhat in the manner of Sir William Chamber's Chinese buildings, as an alternative to the design in the Picturesque fashion, giving the appearance of a *cottage orné*, which was carried out on Holland's behalf by his assistant P. F. Robinson.

18. (p. 68) When explaining to Lady Bessborough how he came to 'get rid of the French things' when he adopted the Chinese style at the Pavilion, the Prince Regent told her he was afraid that his very furniture 'might be accused of Jacobinism'.

Fig. 11. Engraving after a drawing by Tatham of a marble frieze in the Villa Albani, near Rome.

BIBLIOGRAPHY

The Artist's Assistant, 1801.

M. P. BALE, *Woodworking Machinery*, 1923.

S. BAUMGARTEN, *Thomas Hope*, Paris, 1958.

GEOFFREY DE BELLAIGUE, with JOHN RUSSELL, JOHN HARRIS and OLIVER MILLAR, *Buckingham Palace*, 1969.

'Brighton, The Royal Pavilion', Catalogues of the Regency Exhibitions, 1946 and following years.

RICHARD BROWN, *The Rudiments of Drawing Cabinet and Upholstery Furniture . . . after the manner of the antique*, 1820; 2nd edition, 1822.

COMTE DE CAYLUS, *Recueil d'antiquités égyptiennes, étrusques, grecques et romaines*, 7 vols., 1752–67.

P. H. CLAYDEN, *Early Life of Samuel Rogers*, 1887.

ANTHONY COLERIDGE, 'The work of George Bullock, cabinet-maker, in Scotland', articles in the *Connoisseur*, May and June 1965.

M. E. J. DELÉCLUZE, *Louis David, son école et son temps*, Paris, 1855.

VIVANT DENON, *Voyages dans la Basse et la Haute Egypte*, London, 1802.

Dictionary of National Biography.

CARLE DREYFUS, *Le mobilier français*, Paris, 1921.

MARIA EDGEWORTH, *Life and Letters*, 2 vols, 1894.

The Edinburgh Review, July 1807.

RALPH EDWARDS, (i) *The Dictionary of English Furniture*, 3 vols., 1954.

(ii) 'The last phase of Regency design', article in *The Burlington Magazine*, Vol. lxxi, 1937, p. 267.

RALPH EDWARDS and MARGARET JOURDAIN, *Georgian Cabinet-Makers*, 1946.

REV. IRWIN ELLER, *History of Belvoir*, 1841.

RALPH FASTNEDGE, *English Furniture Styles, from 1500 to 1830*, 1955.

RONALD FLEMING, 'Rooms', article in *The Saturday Book*, 1959.

Gentleman's Magazine, November 1806; January 1818.

J. G. GROHMANN, *Remains of Egyptian Architecture*, Leipzig, 1799.

JOSEPH GWILT, *Dictionary of Architecture*, the Architectural Publication Society, 8 vols, 1842.

BIBLIOGRAPHY

R. E. M. HARDING, *History of the Pianoforte*, Cambridge, 1933.

JOHN HARRIS, *Regency Furniture Designs, 1803–1826*, 1961.

H. HAVARD, *Dictionnaire de l'ameublement*, Vol. 1, Paris, 1887.

THOMAS HOPE, *Household Furniture and Interior Decoration*, 1807.

THERLE HUGHES, 'Furniture design of the Regency', article in *Antiques Review*, No. 2, 1949.

CHRISTOPHER HUSSEY, articles in *Country Life*, 14 April 1950, 27 December 1956, 23 January 1958, 26 May 1960.

M. JOURDAIN, (i) *English Interiors in Smaller Houses from the Restoration to the Regency, 1660 to 1830*, Country Life, 1923.

 (ii) *Regency Furniture, 1795–1830*, revised and enlarged by Ralph Fastnedge, 1965.

M. JOURDAIN and R. EDWARDS, *Georgian Cabinet-Makers*, Country Life, 1946.

E. T. JOY, 'Regency Furniture', article in the *Connoisseur* Period Guides: *The Regency Period, 1810–1830*, 1958.

H. W. and I. LAW, *Book of the Beresford Hopes*, 1925.

HECTOR LEFUEL, (i) *Georges Jacob*, Paris, 1923.

 (ii) *Jacob Desmalter*, Paris, 1926.

D. LEDOUX-LEBARD, *Les ébénistes Parisiens, 1795 à 1830*, Paris, 1951.

The London Cabinet-makers' Union book of prices, 1811.

J. C. LOUDON, *Encyclopaedia of Cottage, Farm and Villa Architecture and Furniture*, 1833.

T. MARTIN, *The Circle of the Mechanical Arts*, 1813; 2nd ed., 1820.

HYATT MAYOR, *Piranesi*, New York, 1953.

MARY RUSSELL MITFORD, *Our Village*, ed. G. Whitaker, 5 vols, 1824–32.

HENRY MOSES, (i) *Designs for Antique Vases, Altars, Paterae, Tripods and Candelabra*, 1812.

 (ii) *Designs of Modern Costume*, 1823.

CLIFFORD MUSGRAVE, *Royal Pavilion: an Episode in the Romantic*, 1959.

PETER and MICHAEL ANGELO NICHOLSON, *The Practical Cabinet Maker, Upholsterer and Complete Decorator*, 1826.

JEAN NICOLAY, *Maîtres ébénistes français*, Paris, 1956.

CHARLES PACKER, *Paris Furniture by the Master Ébénists*, 1956.

C. PERCIER and P. F. L. FONTAINE, *Recueil des décorations intérieures*, 1812.

G. B. PIRANESI, (i) *Diversi manieri d'adornare i camini*, 1769.

 (ii) *Vasi, candelabri, sarcofagi, tripodi, lucerne, ed ornamenti antichi*, 1778.

C. L. RANSOM, *Ancient Furniture*, Chicago, 1905.

BRYAN READE, *Regency Antiques*, 1953.

REES, *Cyclopaedia of the Arts and Sciences*, 1819.

The Repository of Arts, etc., R. Ackermann, 1809–28.

GEORGE RICHARDSON, *Collection of Ornaments in the Antique Style*, 1816.

EDWARD F. RIMBAULT, *The Pianoforte*, 1860.

F. ROE, *Windsor Chairs*, 1953.

F. DE SALVERTE, *Les ébénistes du XVIIIᵉ siècle*, Paris, 1934.

ROBERT SAYER, *The Ladies' Amusement*, c. 1758.

THOMAS SHERATON, (i) *The Cabinet-Maker and Upholsterer's Drawing Book*, 1791–4.
>   (ii) *Appendix to The Cabinet-Maker and Upholsterer's Drawing Book*, 1802.
>   (iii) *The Cabinet Dictionary*, 1803.
>   (iv) *The Cabinet-Maker, Upholsterer and General Artist's Encyclopaedia*, 1804–6.
>   (v) *Designs for Household Furniture*, 1812.

G. A. SIDDONS, *The Cabinet-Maker's Guide*, 1830.

H. CLIFFORD SMITH, *Buckingham Palace*, 1931.

GEORGE SMITH, (i) *A Collection of Designs for Household Furniture and Interior Decoration*, 1808.
>   (ii) *A Collection of Ornamental Designs after the Antique*, 1812.
>   (iii) *The Cabinet-Maker's and Upholsterer's Guide*, 1828.

ROBERT SOUTHEY, *Letters from England*, 1957.

Southill: a Regency House, 1951.

DOROTHY STROUD, *Henry Holland, His Life and Architecture*, 1966.

Styles de France: objets et collections, Paris, 1955.

CHARLES HEATHCOTE TATHAM, *Examples of Grecian and Roman Architectural Ornament*, 1799; 4th ed. 1826; republished 1843.

JOHN TAYLOR, *Upholsterer's and Cabinet Maker's Pocket Assistant*, c. 1825.

JOHN TIMBS, *Curiosities of London*, 1857.

The Torrington Diaries, 1781–4, 4 vols., 1934–8.

P. VERLET, (i) *Le mobilier royal français*, 1945.
>   (ii) *Les meubles français du XVIIIᵉ siècle*, 2 vols., 1956.

HORACE WALPOLE, *Letters*, ed. Peter Cunningham, 1906.

WALPOLE SOCIETY, *Transactions*, 1951.

DAVID WATKIN, *Thomas Hope and the Neo-classical Idea*, 1769–1831, 1968.

F. J. B. WATSON, (i) Catalogue of furniture in the Wallace Collection, 1958.
>   (ii) 'The furniture and decorations', in *Southill: a Regency House*, 1951.

(iii) *Louis XVI Furniture*, 1960.

LORD GERALD WELLESLEY (now Duke of Wellington), 'Regency furniture', article in *The Burlington Magazine*, 1937, p. 233.

C. M. WESTMACOTT, *British Galleries of Painting and Sculpture*, 1824.

HENRY WHITAKER, *Designs of Cabinet and Upholstery Furniture in the Most Modern Style*, 1825.

INDEX

In the case of articles of furniture and decorative motifs only the principle references are indexed, because of the multitude of references to such items throughout the work.

MORNING WALKING DRESS.

1. Fashion plate, from Ackermann's *Repository of Arts*, 1813, showing a table from a classical design by Tatham.

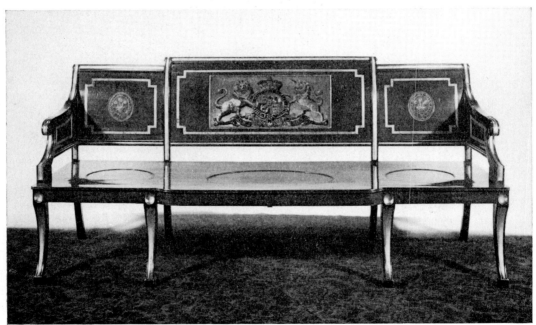

2A. Pier-table from Carlton House, ebony and ormolu, probably by Weisweiler, *c.* 1780.

By gracious permission of H.M. The Queen.

2B. Hall settee, mahogany, painted and gilt, made by Elward, Marsh and Tatham for the Royal Pavilion, 1802.

By gracious permission of H.M. The Queen.

3. Arm-chair, gilt, from the Drawing-room, Southill, *c.* 1796–9, and footstool, *c.* 1807–10.

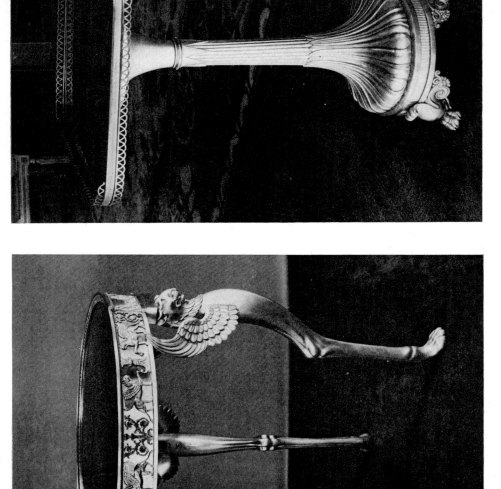

4B. Occasional table, kingwood and gilt, with Egyptian ornament, and profuse scrolling of feet, made for Southill, c. 1812–15.

4A. Circular table, gilt, on winged-lion monopodia supports, similar to a design by Tatham, c. 1800.

5. Furniture from the Drawing-room, Southill, exhibited at the Royal Pavilion, 1951, showing gilt arm-chairs, c. 1796–9, from Southill (with bolt-heads) and from Hartwell (with fluted sides).

6. Furniture from Mrs. Whitbread's Room at Southill, exhibited at the Royal Pavilion, 1951, showing chairs of Louis Seize inspiration, *c.* 1796–99, and chiffoniers, *c.* 1800; tambour-top writing-table, inscribed 1811.

7. Writing-desk, mahogany, in the Sheraton manner, with oval ends and lion-paw feet, c. 1803.

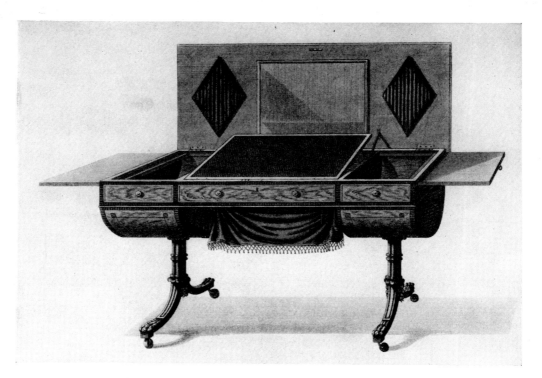

8A. Design for a Lady's Dressing Table, from Sheraton's *Cabinet Dictionary*, 1803.

8B. Lady's Dressing Table, in figured mahogany veneer, made to the above design.

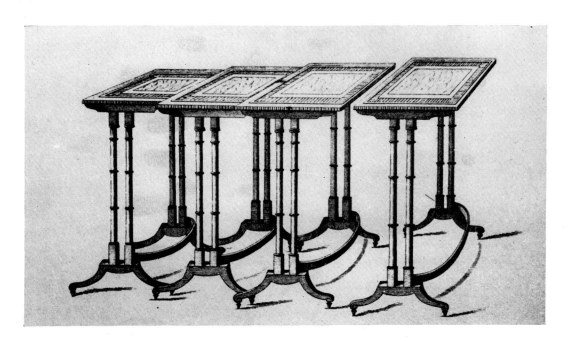

9A. Design by Sheraton for Quartetto Tables, from the *Cabinet Dictionary*, 1803.
9B. Design by Sheraton for a Pembroke Table with cross-supports, from the *Cabinet Dictionary*, 1803.

10. Couch of carved mahogany with shell-back, dolphin-feet and tablet with nautical emblems. Stamped C. Munro. c. 1805.

11. The Dolphin Furniture, presented to Greenwich Hospital, 1813, in memory of Nelson, exhibited at the Royal Pavilion, 1948.

12B. Grecian chair, with arc-back, painted in the manner of an Etruscan vase, similar to a design by Hope, c. 1807.

12A. Grecian chair, mahogany, with arc-back, similar to a design by Hope, c. 1807.

13. Circular table, mahogany inlaid with ebony and silver, from a design in Hope's *Household Furniture*, 1807, once at Deepdene.

14A. Drawing-room stool, with scroll-ended cross-supports, mahogany and gilt, from a design in Hope's *Household Furniture*, 1807.

14B. Dwarf bookcase, rosewood and gilt, with decoration of stars and Egyptian terminal figures, *c.* 1810.

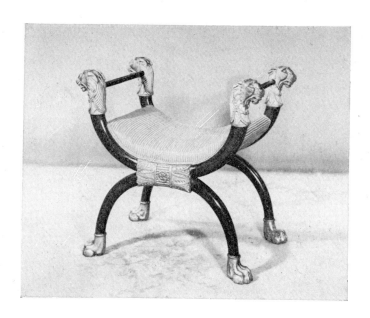

15A. Drawing-room stool, cross-framed, with lion-heads and feet and lotus-leaf
ornament, from a design in Hope's *Household Furniture*, 1807.
15B. Pier-table, of carved and gilt wood, in the manner of one made by G. Jacob
for Malmaison, as illustrated in Hope's *Household Furniture*, 1807. (Compare
Fig. 5.)

16A. Drawing-room stool, in the Egyptian taste, cross-framed, ebonised and gilt, with lotus and ball finials, *c.* 1805.

16B. Commode, in the Egyptian taste, mahogany, with crocodile ornament in bronze, from Embury Park. *c.* 1810.

17. Bookcase-commode, mahogany and gilt, with Egyptian ornament, *c.* 1805.

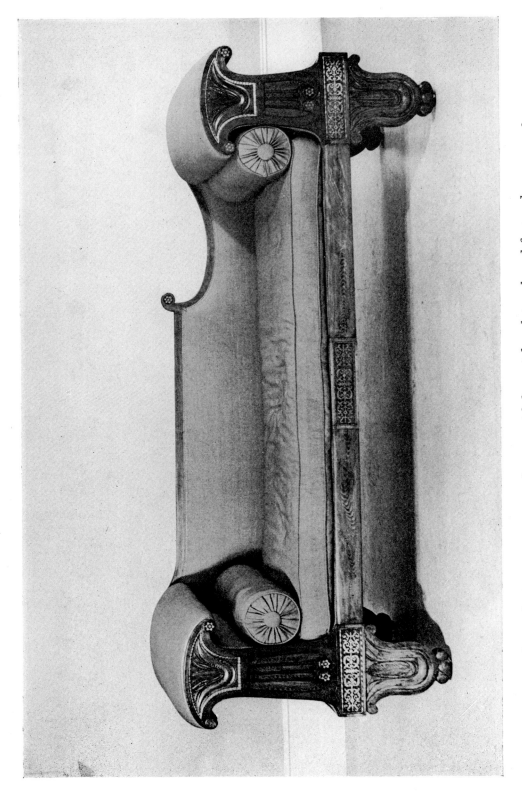

18. Sofa, in the Egyptian taste, mahogany with brass-inlay, lotus-shaped feet and arms, c. 1815.

19. Writing-table, figured mahogany, the side-pedestals shaped as pylons, from a design in Hope's *Household Furniture*, 1807. (Compare Fig. 8.)

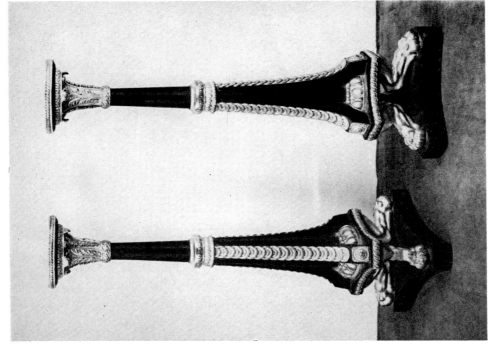

20B. Pair of pedestals, painted and gilt, with lion-feet, in the manner of George Smith, c. 1808.

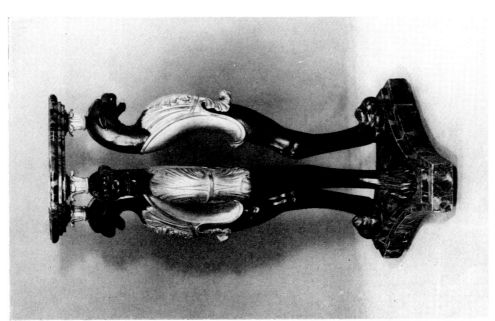

20A. Tripod stand, ebonised and gilt, with lion-monopodia supports, in the manner of George Smith, c. 1808.

21. Couch and arm-chairs in the Egyptian taste, as illustrated in Hope's *Household Furniture*, 1807.

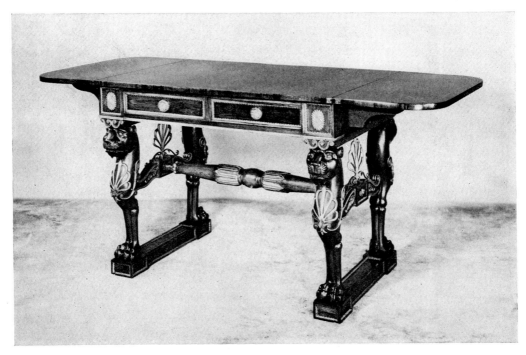

22A. Design for a Sofa-table, with lion-monopodia supports, from George
Smith's *Household Furniture*, 1808.
22B. Sofa-table, rosewood and gilt, made after the design above, *c.* 1808.

23. Designs for Chiffoniers, one in Gothic style, from George Smith's *Household Furniture*, 1808.

24A. Small commode, beech painted as bamboo, with Japanese lacquer panels, made for the Royal Pavilion, 1802, and Chinese export arm-chairs, bamboo, c. 1800.
24B. Dwarf bookcase and specimen cabinet, japanned in the Chinese taste, c. 1808.

25. Chiffonier-commode, decorated in Japanese lacquer, with ormolu dragon shelf-supports and gilt wood colonnettes, c. 1815

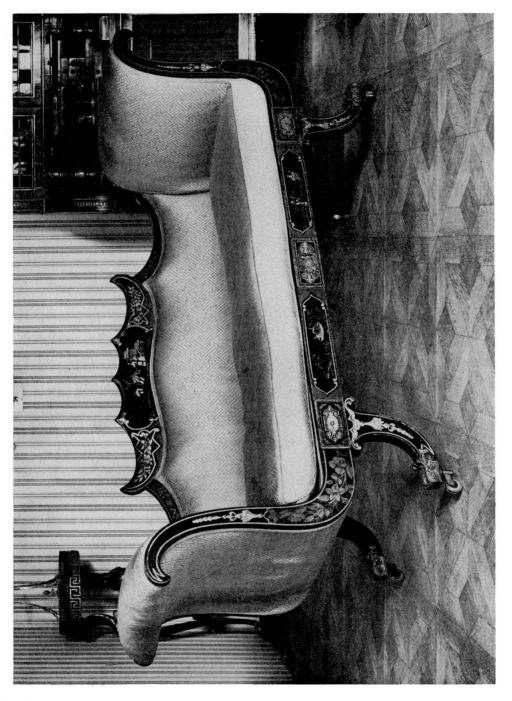

26. Sofa, in the Chinese taste, japanned black and gold, the back-rail shaped with a 'pagoda-roof' motif, c. 1815.

27. Suite of bedroom furniture, of beech painted to simulate bamboo, from Dorneywood, c. 1815. Exhibited at the Royal Pavilion, 1951.

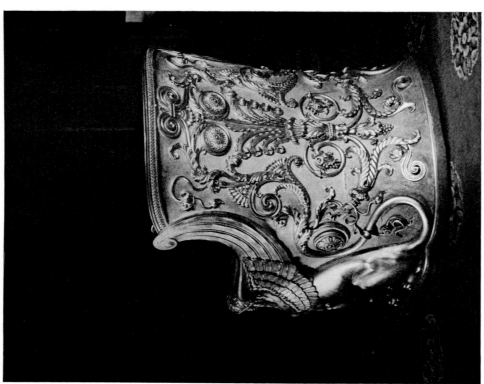

28B. Rear view of the same, showing luxuriant foliate ornament.

By gracious permission of H.M. The Queen.

28A. Council chair, carved and gilt wood, one of a pair made for Carlton House, c. 1813, probably from a design by Tatham.

29. Drawing-room table, amboyna, on carved and gilt wood dolphin supports, and stylised ormolu lion-paw feet, c. 1812.

30. Writing-table, kingwood and gilt, the base carved with bold scrolling, made for Southill, *c.* 1812–15.

31. Circular drawing-room table, kingwood and gilt, with bold scrolling and foliate ornament, made for Southill, c. 1812–15.

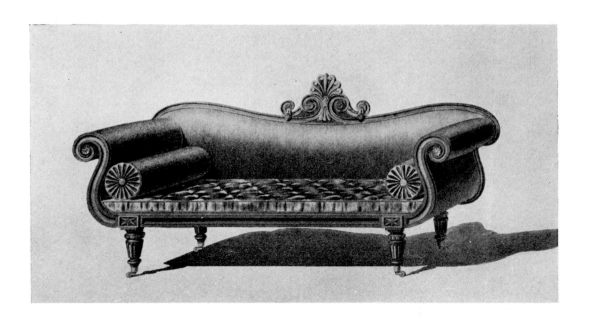

32A. Design for a sofa, with straight turned legs and boldly carved back-crest, by Michael Angelo Nicholson, from *The Practical Cabinet-Maker*, 1826.

32B. Design for a sideboard and sarcophagus cellaret, by Michael Angelo Nicholson, from *The Practical Cabinet-Maker*, 1826.

33A. Design for a console table, 'after the style of Louis XIV', from George Smith's *Cabinet-Maker's Guide*, 1828.

33B. Design for a wardrobe, from George Smith's *Cabinet-Maker's Guide*, 1828.

34B. Tea-poy, containing caddies, with late type 'all-over' buhl-work of *chinoiserie* design, *c.* 1820.

34A. Worktable on pedestal, coromandel wood, with early type brass-inlay in detached 'Chinese' motifs, *c.* 1808.

35. Octagonal drawing-room table, amboyna, with brass-inlay of flower and leaf design, in the manner of G. Bullock, c. 1818.

36. Dwarf bookcase-commode, mahogany, with flower and leaf-pattern buhl-work; gilt metal human masks and plinth in Louis Quatorze manner, c. 1820.

37. Commode, ebonised, with painted classical ornament, and flower paintings in the manner of Jacob-Desmalter, in Louis Quatorze style surrounds, c. 1826.

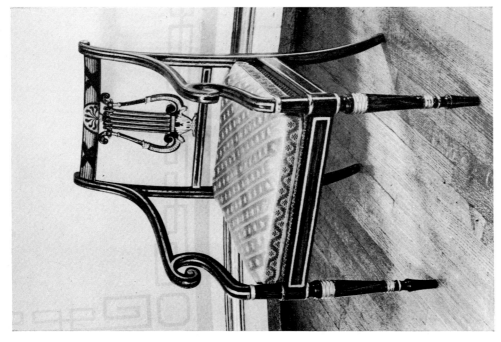

38B. Arm-chair with scrolled arm-supports and scroll-back, painted as rosewood and gilt, c. 1805.

38A. Grecian arc-back chair, ebonised and gilt, with crossed front-supports, c. 1805.

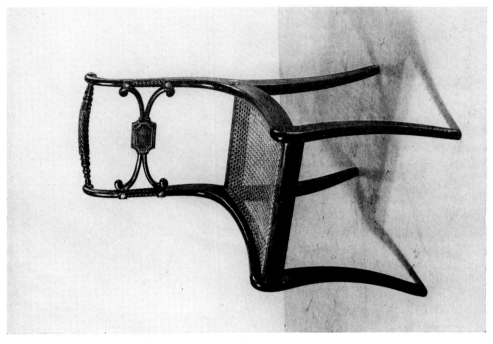

39B. Trafalgar parlour-chair with curved sides, scimitar-legs and rope moulding to back-rail and back-supports. Originally painted black, c. 1805.

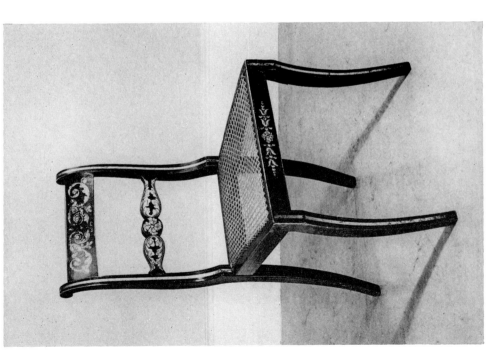

39A. Parlour-chair with scroll-back and square-section swept legs and straight seat-rails. Beech, painted black and gilt, c. 1805.

40. Parlour-chairs, mahogany, the backs carved with volutes, reeded Trafalgar legs, and scrolled arms, *c.* 1812.

41B. Library chair, mahogany inlaid with ebony, the arms carved with rams'-heads, the arc-back outswept, c. 1812.

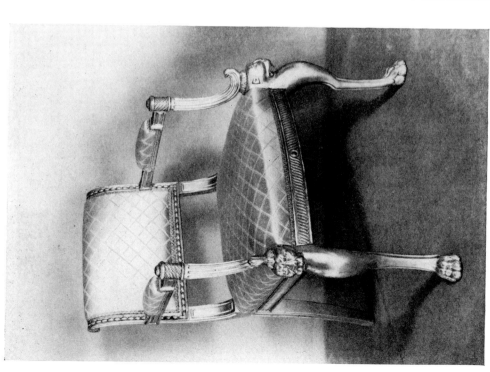

41A. Drawing-room arm-chair, gilt, with lion-monopodia front legs, and scroll-back, c. 1808.

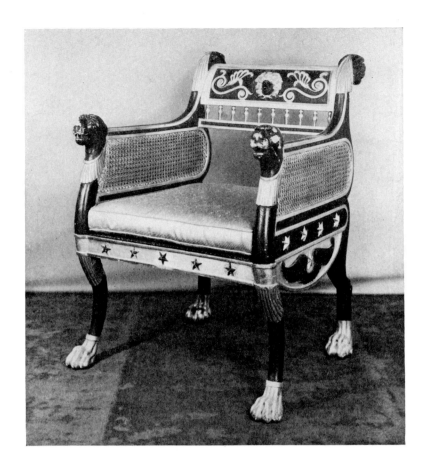

42A. Drawing-room arm-chair, with lion-headed arm and back-supports and
lion-feet, in the manner of George Smith. Painted and gilt, c. 1808.

42B. Two footstools, one of console design, carved and gilt, c. 1815, one of
rosewood with gilt metal honeysuckle-shaped feet, c. 1812.

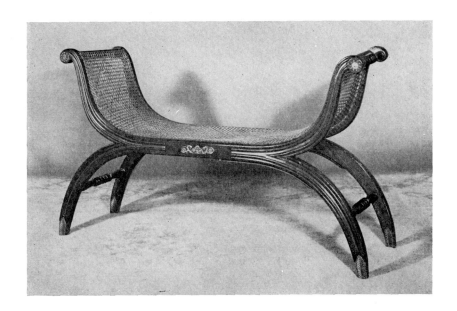

43A. Window-seat, mahogany, with scrolled and reeded supports, and gilt metal ornaments, *c*. 1810.

43B. Windsor garden-chair, with cross-frame legs, and original painted decoration of drab and blue, *c*. 1810.

44. Two bedroom chairs, beech, carved and painted to simulate bamboo, *c.* 1815.

45B. Bedroom chair, with 'tablet back', 'painted drab and blue' to represent bamboo, made for the Royal Pavilion, c. 1802. (Restored.)

45A. Chair, simulating bamboo, with Gothic quatrefoil fret in back-rail, made by Elward, Marsh and Tatham for the Royal Pavilion, 1802.

46A. Sofa, painted as rosewood and gilt, in the French taste, *c.* 1812.
46B. Grecian sofa, mahogany and canework, double-ended, with centre-cresting to back-rail, *c.* 1820.

47A. Sofa, painted and gilt, with typical mid-Regency classical decoration,
c. 1811–15.

47B. Settee, carved and gilt, with centre-cresting in form of scrolls and shell to
back-rail, made by Morel and Seddon for Windsor Castle, 1829.

By gracious permission of H.M. The Queen.

48. French commode, mahogany, tapering fluted columns with concave hollowing at tops, peg-top feet, marked Weisweiler, c. 1780. The prototype of many English Regency pieces.

49. Commode, mahogany and gilt, the English interpretation of Louis Seize models, c. 1805.

50B. Dwarf commode in French Empire manner, with brass grille doors and marble columns, c. 1815.

50A. Dwarf commode, coromandel wood, with tapering colonnettes and peg-top feet, in Louis Seize manner, with brass grille doors, c. 1805.

51. Dwarf bookcase, painted bronze-green and gilt, following closely the spirit of Louis Seize commodes, c. 1805.

52A. Pair of small pier-tables, rosewood with gilt metal ornaments and white
marble tops, scroll-shaped supports, *c.* 1815.
52B. Pier-table, rosewood with carved and gilt wood ornaments and columns,
the latter with lotus-leaf ornament, *c.* 1812.

53. Commode-chiffonier, rosewood, with gadrooned bun-feet and carved leaf-ornament, *c.* 1820.

54. Large commode-chiffonier, rosewood, with ormolu mounts, c. 1812–15.

55. Bookcase-commode, rosewood, scagliola top, gilt Corinthian pilasters, the frieze decoration painted on porcelain, the door and end-panels painted with figure-subjects from Herculaneum, *c.* 1815.

56. China-cabinet, one of a pair, rosewood cross-banded with satinwood, gilt colonnettes and peg-top feet, *c.* 1810.

57. Cabinet, rosewood and gilt, in the Southill manner, decorated with small panels of painted Chinese porcelain, *c.* 1800.

58. Sofa-table, mahogany, with straight end-supports, c. 1800.

59. Sofa-table, mahogany, with platform base and turned column centre-supports, *c.* 1810.

60. Top of sofa-table, decorated with a classical scene in penwork, c. 1810.

61. Sofa-table, on lyre-shaped end-supports, ebonised and decorated with classical designs in penwork, c. 1810.

62. Sofa-table, mahogany, with early type brass-inlay decoration in detached motifs, and turned central pedestal-support, c. 1812–15.

63. Sofa-table, amboyna, with brass-inlay of running scroll design, platform-base and centre pedestal-support, made about 1816 for Claremont, Esher, Surrey, home of the Princess Charlotte.

By gracious permission of H.M. The Queen.

64. Sofa-table, amboyna, with gilt mounts, the base capped with rosettes. Bears label of T. and C. Seddon. c. 1833-7.

65. Card-table, in satinwood and rosewood, on centre pedestal and scroll-supports, c. 1812.

66B. Music-canterbury, rosewood, of lyre design, with column-supports, c. 1810.

66A. Pot-stand, mahogany, on tripod-base carved as dolphins, c. 1815.

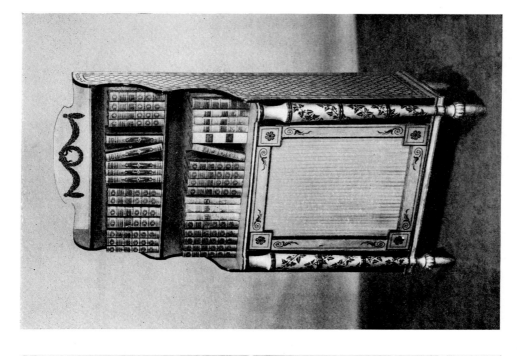

67B. Small occasional bookcase-cupboard, with Louis Seize pattern tapering pilasters and peg-top feet, painted, c. 1810.

67A. Small occasional bookcase with lyre-shaped ends, c. 1805.

68. Library bookcase, rosewood, of early classical design, with diamond-shaped 'Directoire' decoration, *c.* 1805.

69. Library bookcase, mahogany, of late classical design, with heavily carved scroll-pediment, *c.* 1826.

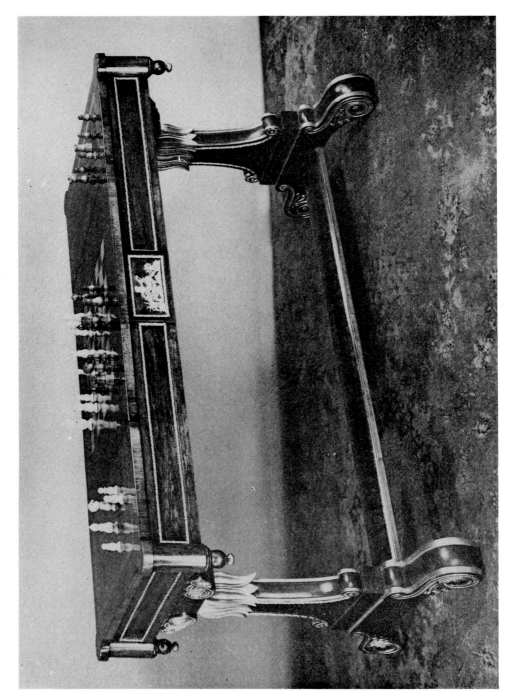

70. Large writing-games-table, with ormolu mounts of lotus-leaves, and scrolling at feet, *c.* 1815.

71. Large circular library-table, mahogany, with pilaster supports in the Egyptian taste, c. 1808.

72. Octagonal library-table, satinwood and gilt, in the later Southill manner, made for William Lee Antonie of Colworth, c. 1812–15. Later at Hartwell House.

73. Circular library-table, pollarded oak, on triangular pedestal, c. 1815.

74. Carlton House writing-desk, rosewood, with tassel-top legs, made for Carlton House, c. 1810.

By gracious permission of H.M. The Queen.

75. Writing-table, mahogany, with late type turned and reeded legs and leaf-ornament, c. 1820.

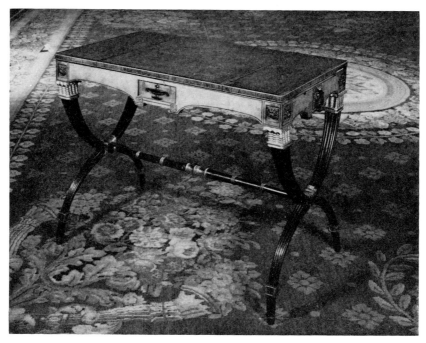

76A. Small writing-table, mahogany, on lyre-shaped supports,
and with 'bobbin' type corners, *c.* 1810.
76B. Small writing-table, with cross-framed and reeded supports.
Bears label of John Maclean and Sons. *c.* 1810.

77A. Circular dwarf bookcase, rosewood, with gilt mouldings and
mounts, c. 1810.

77B. Map-cabinet, mahogany, with stand painted black and bronze-
green, in form deriving from a design by Tatham, c. 1810.

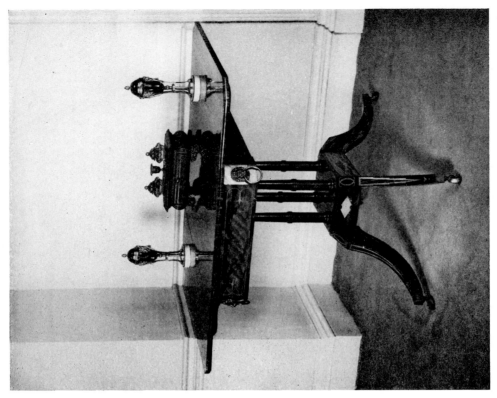

78B. Pembroke-table, coromandel wood, on four central column-supports and claw-base, c. 1810.

78A. *Bonheur-de-jour* writing-desk, rosewood and gilt, the legs turned with 'bamboo' rings, stamped E. Butler, c. 1804.

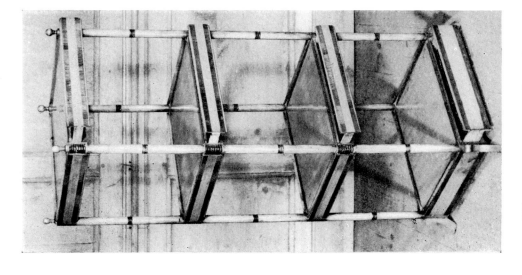

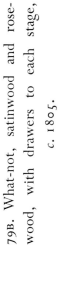

79B. What-not, satinwood and rose-wood, with drawers to each stage, c. 1805.

79A. Library steps, beech, carved and painted to represent bamboo, c. 1815.

80B. The same, with steps extended.

80A. 'The Patent Metamorphic Library Chair', mahogany, c. 1810.

81. 'Square pianoforte' by Broadwood, mahogany cross-banded with rosewood, heavily reeded turned legs, c. 1815–20.

82. Cottage sideboard in Gothic taste, mahogany with ebony inlay, *c.* 1810, and clock in Gothic case, *c.* 1815.

83. Small sideboard, mahogany, in the Egyptian taste, *c. 1805*.

84. Sideboard-table, one of a pair, mahogany, with ebonised lion-monopodia supports, c. 1810, and oval sarcophagus wine-cellaret, c. 1810.

85. Large sideboard, kingwood, with brass inlay of classical design, and high pedestal cupboards, c. 1810.

86. Dining-table, mahogany, with framed top-sections, on pillar-and-claw supports, c. 1815.

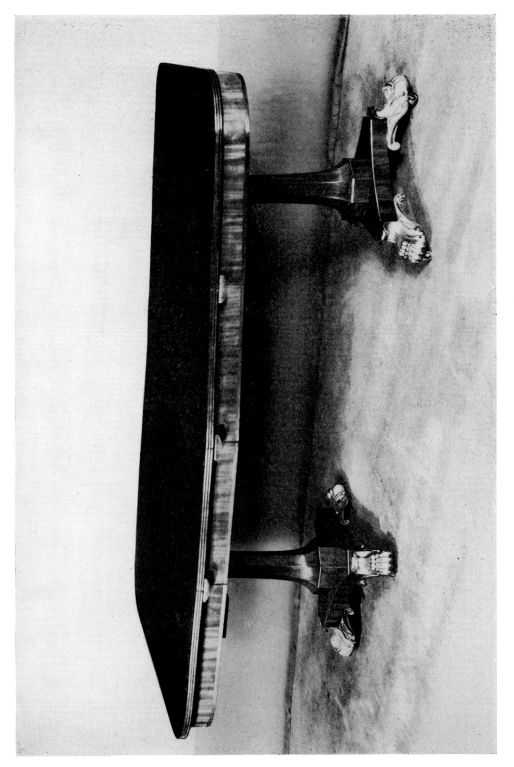

87. Dining-table, mahogany, with framed top-sections, on pedestal-and-tablet supports, *c.* 1826.

88B. Circular marble-topped table, with brass-inlay in re-peated motifs, on gilt pedestal, c. 1820.

88A. Occasional table, rosewood and gilt, with divided-column supports, c. 1808.

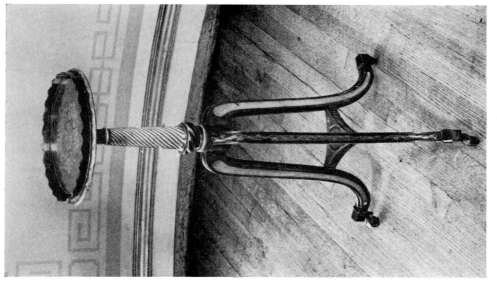

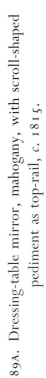

89B. Pedestal on tripod standard base, c. 1803.

89A. Dressing-table mirror, mahogany, with scroll-shaped pediment as top-rail, c. 1815.

90B. Chest of drawers, mahogany, with bold late pattern scroll-ornament, c. 1826.

90A. Chest of drawers, mahogany and satinwood, with classical inlay, c. 1803.

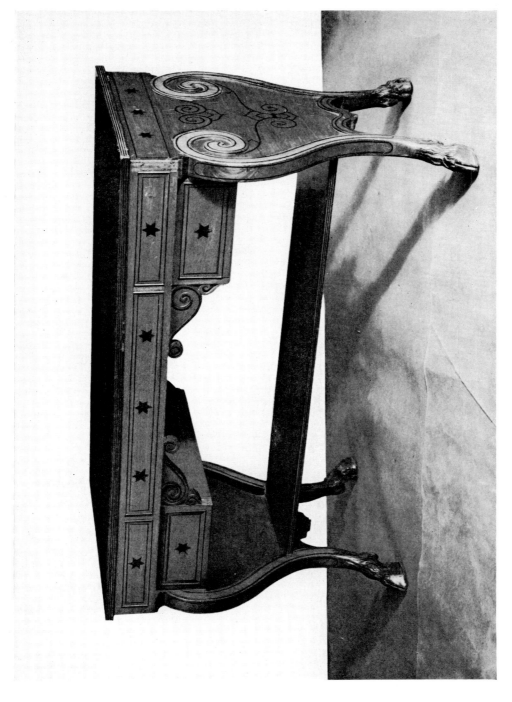

91. Dressing-table, mahogany inlaid with ebony, and console-supports similar to a design by Smith, and deriving from a design by Tatham, c. 1808.

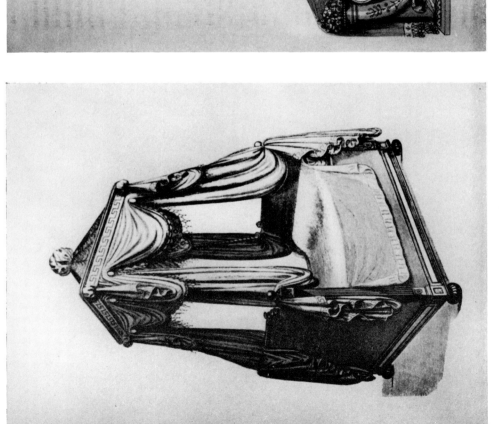

92A. Design for a French sofa-bed, from Sheraton's *Cabinet Encyclopaedia*, 1804, republished 1812.

92B. Design for a French sofa-bed, from Ackermann's *Repository of Arts*, November, 1822.

93. A bedroom in the Chinese taste at the Royal Pavilion, with painted canopy-bed and washing-stand, c. 1815, and Chinese export chairs, c. 1802.

94. Convex wall-mirror, with finely modelled leaf-decoration, *c.* 1803.

95A. Overmantel mirror, with three glasses, gilt, with classical decoration in relief, c. 1810.

95B. Overmantel mirror, gilt, with romantic landscape decoration painted under glass, c. 1815.

96. Revolving bookcase, mahogany, with painted classical decoration, *c.* 1807.